I

# THE YOGA OF SLEEP AND DREAMS

# THE YOGA OF
# SLEEP AND DREAMS

## THE NIGHT-SCHOOL OF SADHANA

*Selections from the Works of*
SRI AUROBINDO
*and*
THE MOTHER

*Compiled with an Introduction by*
A. S. Dalal

**SRI AUROBINDO ASHRAM
PONDICHERRY**

First edition 2004
Second impression 2008

Rs 50
ISBN 978-81-7058-750-7

© Sri Aurobindo Ashram Trust 2004
Published by Sri Aurobindo Ashram Publication Department,
Pondicherry 605 002
Web    http://www.sabda.in
Printed at Sri Aurobindo Ashram Press, Pondicherry
PRINTED IN INDIA

Sadhana can go on in the dream or sleep state as well as in the waking.

**SRI AUROBINDO**
(*Letters on Yoga*, SABCL, Vol. 24, p.1481)

Once one is in full sadhana, sleep becomes as much a part of it as waking.

**SRI AUROBINDO**
(*Letters on Yoga*, SABCL, Vol. 24, p.1481)

*Mother, what is sleep? Is it only the need of the body to rest or is it something else?*

Sleep can be a very active means of concentration and inner knowledge. Sleep is the school one has to go through, if one knows how to learn his lesson there, so that the inner being may be independent of the physical form, conscious in itself and master of its own life. There are entire parts of the being which need this immobility and semi-consciousness of the outer being, of the body, in order to be able to live their own life, independently.

Only, people don't know, they sleep because they sleep, as they eat, as they live — by a kind of instinct, a semi-conscious impulse. They don't even ask themselves the question. You are asking the question now: Why does one sleep? But there are millions and millions of beings who sleep without ever having asked themselves the question why one sleeps. They sleep because they feel sleepy, they eat because they are hungry, and they do foolish things because their instincts push them, without thinking, without reasoning; but for those who know, sleep is a school, an excellent school for something other than the school of waking hours.

It is another school for another purpose, but it is a school. If one wants to make the maximum progress possible, one must know how to use one's nights as one uses one's days; only, usually people don't at all know what to do, and they try to remain awake and all that they create is a physical and vital imbalance — and sometimes a mental one also — as a result.

THE MOTHER

(*Questions and Answers 1955*, CWM, Vol. 7, pp. 70-71)

# CONTENTS

# PREFACE

A rare and rich treasure among the spiritual discoveries of world-teachers down the ages lies in the largely unknown wisdom about sleep and dreams which is to be found in the teachings of Sri Aurobindo and the Mother. This book represents a distillation of these teachings.

In common parlance, dreams figuratively signify things which are unreal, for to our ordinary consciousness the world of reality is what we experience in the waking state; what we experience in the dream state is regarded by us as an unreal phantasmagoria which is usually chaotic and seemingly devoid of any real significance. Western psychology, beginning with Freud and continuing with Jung, has thrown some light on the meaning of dreams. As a result, we now understand at least to some extent the significance of dreams and what they can reveal about elements of our nature which are largely concealed to our conscious awareness. But whereas some progress has been made in understanding the *meaning* of dreams, the *nature* of dreams still eludes us. Thus, Arthur S. Reber, author of the *Penguin Dictionary of Psychology*, remarking that "a lot of people have wrestled" with the definition of dream, suggests that we settle for "images during sleep" as a definition. Such a whittled down definition is a frank admission of the paucity of our ascertained knowledge about the nature of dreams.

From the viewpoint of the yogic psychology of dreams presented in this book, one chief limitation of our present-day understanding of the nature of dreams lies in its lack of the distinction which yogic psychology makes between dreams and dream-experiences. Dreams, which constitute most of what we ordinarily bring back from sleep to our waking recollection, are products of what Sri Aurobindo calls the subconscient — that part of our constitution which lies between consciousness and total inconscience. Distinguished from these ordinary dreams are dream-experiences which are recordings of transcripts if actual events in supraphysical or inner (subliminal) realms of our existence which are as real and concrete as the physical world if not more so, and into which sleep gives us an entry. "In each we see scenes, meet beings, share in happenings, come across formations, influences, suggestions which belong to these planes. Even when we are awake, part of us moves in these planes, but the activity goes on behind the veil; our waking minds are not aware of it."[1] A dream-experience is a direct or symbolic record of what happens to us in these realms. Unlike the ordinary dreams which come from the subconscient and which are chaotic, confused and tiring, dream-experiences, especially those in the subliminal realms, are clear and coherent (though often mixed and distorted by the subconscient), and produce a deep feeling of insight or elevation. The three early dreams of the Mother in Appendix II are examples of such inner experiences during the dream state. The aim of the yoga of sleep and dreams in the beginning is to replace what is commonly a slumber of subconscious dreams with a sleep of inner experiences. Sleep then becomes as much a part of sadhana as the waking state. The key for being able to continue sadhana during sleep lies in becoming more and more

---

1. Sri Aurobindo, *Letters on Yoga*, SABCL Vol. 24, p. 1500.

conscious, not only during the waking hours but also during sleep. The fact that one can become conscious during sleep has been known to yogis since ancient times, but it is only during the past few decades that scientific psychology has been interested in the experience of consciousness during sleep. The interest has been aroused by the phenomenon of what are called "lucid dreams"—dreams in which one knows that one is dreaming.

Jayne Gackenbach, one of the foremost researchers of lucid dreaming, has arrived at a theory, based on studies carried out by herself and others, that lucid dreaming is only the beginning; it is only one step along a developmental continuum of consciousness during sleep, and that there are further steps of development beyond lucid dreaming. She states:

> The potential far-reaching implications of consciousness in sleep are just beginning to be investigated if not appreciated. We are at the entry of a new era in our understanding of such states and their implications for full human functioning.[2]

The psychology of sleep and dreams, founded on yogic experience, contained in the pages of this book illuminates Gackenbach's theory by placing it in a larger and deeper perspective, and indicates the farthest goal of the yoga of sleep and dreams — that of transforming sleep from a state of semi-unconsciousness into a state of yogic repose in

2. Karen Nesbitt Shanor, *The Emerging Mind*, Los Angeles: Renaissance Books, 1999.

which one is as conscious during "sleep" as one is during the waking state. In other words, the highest goal envisaged is to become fully and continuously conscious throughout the day and night, capable of consciously entering the inner worlds of existence at will and acting there, if necessary, as one would act in the physical world. This book also contains guidance for making sleep more and more conscious, thereby progressively replacing subconscient dreams with conscious experiences of the inner realms of our being.

A.S.D.

# INTRODUCTION

## The Role of Sleep and Dreams in the Spiritual Life

"A sleep that imitates death is his repose",[1] writes Sri Aurobindo in describing our ordinary sleep which is characterised by a fall into a state of semi-consciousness and a discontinuity of conscious existence. In contrast to ordinary sleep is the sleep of the yogi in which there is full and unbroken consciousness while the outer being — physical, vital and mental — is in a state of complete repose. The Mother gave a description of such a state in a letter to her son commenting on a newspaper article which stated that the Mother had not slept for several months. She wrote:

> It is true that for a long time I have not slept in the usual sense of the word. That is to say, at no time do I fall into the inconscience which is the sign of ordinary sleep. But I do give my body the rest it needs, that is, two or three hours of lying down in a condition of absolute immobility in which the whole being, mental, psychic, vital and physical, enters into a complete state of rest made of perfect peace, absolute silence and total immobility, while the consciousness remains perfectly awake; or else I enter into an internal activity of one or more states of being, an activity which constitutes the occult work and which, needless to say, is also

---

1. Sri Aurobindo, *Savitri*, Sri Aurobindo Birth Centenary Library (SABCL), Vol. 28, p. 164.

perfectly conscious. So I can say, in all truth, that I
never lose consciousness throughout the twenty-four
hours, which thus form an unbroken sequence, and that
I no longer experience ordinary sleep, while still giving my body the rest that it needs.[2]

Even before one has attained such a consummate yogic state
in which one does not lose consciousness throughout the
twenty-four hours, one can, through sadhana, become progressively conscious during sleep, thereby replacing more
and more the ordinary subconscious slumber with a sleep of
inner experiences, and thus continue sadhana in sleep as
well as during the waking hours.

## Sleep and Its Spiritual Role

Yogic psychology explains the nature of sleep and sleep-
experiences in terms of the nature and operations of consciousness. In the ordinary consciousness, we are aware of
only the physical world through that part of the mind which
is concerned only with physical things and is limited by the
physical view and experience of things. We are not aware of
the greater realms of our inner being because they are put
behind by our waking consciousness, "much as the veil of
the sunlight hides from us the vast worlds of the stars that
are behind it" (pp. 8-9). Regarding this inner or subliminal

2. The Mother, *Some Answers from the Mother*, Collected Works of the
Mother (CWM), Vol. 16, pp. 3-4.

being of which we are not conscious in our waking state, Sri
Aurobindo states:

> Our waking state is unaware of its connection with the
> subliminal being, although it receives from it, — but
> without any knowledge of the place of origin, — the
> inspirations, intuitions, ideas, will-suggestions, sense-
> suggestions, urges to action that rise from below or from
> behind our limited surface existence. Sleep like trance
> opens the gate of the subliminal to us; for in sleep, as
> in trance, we retire behind the veil of the limited wak-
> ing personality and it is behind this veil that the sub-
> liminal has its existence.[3]

In ordinary sleep, one does not become aware of the realms
of the inner being because in ordinary sleep our being is
submerged in the subconscient, that part of us which is intermediate between waking consciousness and pure inconscience. The subconscient, which in the waking state is
overpowered by the conscious mind, comes on the surface
during sleep and consciousness is submerged in it. Thus, in
ordinary sleep, it is the subconscient that is the consciousness in the body.

However, the inner being — subtle physical, vital, mental
and psychic — is not concentrated upon the body during
sleep; it becomes more or less independent and goes to dwell
in its own realms. Thus, for the sadhak, sleep provides an
opportunity for waking up in the inner being and experien-

3. Sri Aurobindo, *The Life Divine*, SABCL, Vol. 18, p. 426.

cing life in the subliminal realms of our being. The need for sleep from the viewpoint of spiritual life is stated by Sri Aurobindo thus:

> This drawing inside [of consciousness during sleep] is necessary because the active mind of the human being [during the waking state] is at first too much turned to outward things; it has to go inside altogether in order to live in the inner being (inner mind, inner vital, inner physical, psychic).[4]

The Mother states the same fact in different words.

> [If prior to falling asleep one can put oneself in a state of total repose — physical, vital and mental] the inner being which is rarely in relation with the outer life, because the outer life is too noisy and too unconscious for it to be able to manifest itself, can become aware of itself and awaken, become active and act upon the lower parts, establish a conscious contact. This is the real reason for sleep, apart from the necessity that, in the present conditions of life, activity and rest, rest and activity must alternate.[5]

## Dreams and Dream-Experiences

As stated above, consciousness normally sinks into the

---

4. Sri Aurobindo, *Letters on Yoga*, SABCL, Vol. 24, p. 1483.
5. The Mother, *Questions and Answers 1955*, CWM, Vol. 7, p. 71.

subconscient which comes on the surface during sleep. The subconscient is a storehouse of past or persistent habits and experiences, all of which leave a mark on it and have a power of recurrence, especially during sleep.

> All that we do, feel or experience in life leaves an impression, a sort of essential memory of itself in the subconscient and this can come up in dreams even long after those feelings, movements or experiences have ceased in the conscious being, — still more when they have been recent and are only now or lately thrown away from the mind or vital.[6]

The subconscient, which comes on the surface during sleep, is the source of ordinary dreams. As Sri Aurobindo explained:

> Normally it is a subconscient part in us, intermediate between consciousness and pure inconscience, that sends up through this surface layer its formations in the shape of dreams, constructions marked by an apparent inconsequence and incoherence. Many of these are fugitive structures built upon circumstances of our present life selected apparently at random and surrounded with a phantasy of variation; others call back the past, or rather selected circumstances and persons of the past, as a starting-point for similar fleeting edifices. There are other dreams of the subconscious which

6. Sri Aurobindo, *Letters on Yoga*, SABCL, Vol. 24, p. 1597.

seem to be pure phantasy without any such initiation
or basis.... (p. 8)

But in sleep a large part of our consciousness does not
sink into the subconscient;

> ...it passes beyond the veil into other planes of being
> which are connected with our own inner planes, planes
> of supraphysical existence, worlds of a larger life, mind
> or psyche which are there behind and whose influences
> come to us without our knowledge. (p. 9)

> In each we see scenes, meet beings, share in happen-
> ings, come across formations, influences, suggestions
> which belong to these planes. Even when we are awake,
> part of us moves in these planes, but their activity goes
> on behind the veil; our waking minds are not aware of
> it. (pp. 10-11)

Dream-experiences, as distinguished from ordinary dreams,
are records — often mixed and distorted — or transcripts of
experiences in these inner worlds. These dream-experiences
of the subliminal planes are altogether different from the
ordinary dreams constructed by the subconscient, though
most people are not aware of the distinction between the
two. As the Mother remarks,

> ...since we usually give the name "dream" to a consid-
> erable number of activities that differ completely from
> one another, the first point is to learn to distinguish

between these various activities — that is, to recognise what part of the being it is that "dreams", what domain it is that one "dreams" in, and what the nature of that activity is.[7]

In passage 48 (page 27) the Mother explains how one can distinguish a dream from a dream-experience.

To reiterate in Sri Aurobindo's words the distinction between ordinary dreams and dream-experiences:

It is the subconscient that is active in the ordinary dreams. But in the dreams in which one goes out into other planes of consciousness, mental, vital, subtle physical, it is part of the inner being, inner mental or vital or physical that is usually active.[8]

When one does sadhana, the subconscient dreams diminish and the subliminal dream-experiences become more common.

### Significance of Dreams

Dreams from the subconscient, "which are the bulk of those remembered by people who live in the external mind mostly"[9], have no meaning, for the transcriptions of the subconscient

7. The Mother, *Some Answers from the Mother*, CWM, Vol. 16, p. 232.
8. Sri Aurobindo, *Letters on Yoga*, SABCL, Vol. 24, p. 1487.
9. Sri Aurobindo, *Letters on Yoga*, SABCL Vol. 24, p. 1496.

> ... are fantastic and often mixed, combining a jumble
> of different elements: some play with impressions from
> the past, some translate outward touches pressing on
> the sleep-mind; most are fragments from successive
> dream experiences that are not really part of one con-
> nected experience — as if a gramophone record were
> to be made up of snatches of different songs all jum-
> bled together. (p. 24)

However, one can learn a good deal from them. As the
Mother states:

> Very few dreams have a meaning, an instructive value,
> but all dreams can show you what your present state of
> consciousness is and how things are combined in the
> subconscious, what the terrestrial influences are, what
> traces they leave and how they are combined.[10]

Dreams from the mental and vital planes are either *experiences*, that is, actual happenings that have taken place in
those planes during sleep, or are *formations*, that is, things
that are created by one's thoughts and feelings during the
waking state and come back in sleep in the form of dreams.
Explaining to a disciple the difference between a happening
or experience and a formation, Sri Aurobindo writes:

> ...this dream was an actual happening on the vital plane,
> not a formation. If somebody attacks you in the street,

---

10. The Mother, *Words of the Mother*, CWM, Vol. 15, p. 349.

that is not a formation. But if somebody hypnotises you and suggests that you are ill — that suggestion is a formation put in by the hypnotiser. (p. 26)

Regarding the nature of a formation dream, the Mother states:

On the mental plane all the formations made by the mind — the actual "forms" that it gives to the thoughts — return and appear to you as if they were coming from outside and give you dreams. Most dreams are like that. Some people have a very conscious mental life and are able to enter the mental plane and move about in it with the same independence they have in physical life; these people have mentally objective nights. But most people are incapable of doing this: it is their mental activity going on during sleep and assuming forms, and these forms give them what they call dreams.

There is a very common example — it is amusing because it is rather vivid. If you have quarrelled with someone during the day, you may wish to hit him, to say very unpleasant things to him. You control yourself, you don't do it, but your thought, your mind is at work and in your sleep you suddenly have a terrible dream. Someone approaches you with a stick and you hit each other and have a real fight. And when you wake up, if you don't know, if you don't understand what has happened, you say to yourself, 'What an unpleasant dream I had!' But in fact it is your own thought which came back to you, like that. (p. 29)

Sri Aurobindo throws further light on formation dreams:

> Sometimes they are the formations of your own mind
> or vital; sometimes they are the formations of other
> minds with an exact or modified transcription in yours;
> sometimes formations come that are made by the non-
> human forces or beings of these other planes.[11]

As stated previously, subliminal dreams are records or transcripts of experiences in the inner planes — inner or subtle
physical, inner vital, inner mental and the psychic. When
these experiences are transcribed through the subconscient
in the brain in the form of images, impressions, words,
thoughts and feelings, and translated by the mind perfectly
or imperfectly, we remember them as dreams. What we remember are not the actual experiences but only a transcription and interpretation of the experiences. The Mother gives
the following example of a transcription:

> ... a writer was preoccupied with a half-written chap-
> ter which he was unable to finish.
>     His mind, particularly interested in this work of com-
> position, continued the chapter during the night, and
> the more it phrased and rephrased the ideas making up
> the various paragraphs, it became aware that these ideas
> were not expressed in the most rational order and that

11. Sri Aurobindo, *Letters on Yoga*, SABCL, Vol. 24, p. 1488.

the paragraphs had to be rearranged.

All this work was transcribed in the consciousness of our writer in the following dream: he was in his study with several armchairs which he had just brought there and was arranging and rearranging them in the room, until he found the most suitable place for each one.[12]

Subliminal dreams, unlike subconscient dreams, are coherent, but since they are usually disguised and symbolic transcriptions rather than true records of subliminal experiences, the interpretation of subliminal dreams calls for much study of one's sleep experiences. If one can learn to understand one's dreams, all sleep experiences, including subconscient dreams, dreams from the vital and mental planes, and subliminal dreams, "can have a great value in them and convey truths that are not so easy to get in the waking state." (pp. 42-43)

### Sleep — Doorway to Worlds Within

The spiritual value of sleep, however, does not depend solely on one's ability to understand one's dreams. As previously stated, sleep is a going inward and entering inner realms of our being which we are not aware of in our waking state because the physical consciousness which dominates our waking state is too much turned to things of the outer world.

12. The Mother, *Words of Long Ago*, CWM, Vol. 2, pp. 33-34.

Thus, "sleep gives us a right of secret entry" (p. 20) to deeper parts of our being which are normally sealed to our waking consciousness. In ordinary sleep, in which the being is submerged in the subconscient, we do not become aware of these deeper parts of our being. But if one can learn to make sleep more and more conscious,

> ...sleep changes into an inner mode of consciousness in which the sadhana can continue as much as in the waking state, and at the same time one is able to enter into other planes of consciousness than the physical and command an immense range of informative and utilisable experience.[13]

Sleep is a valuable opportunity to become conscious within because it is easier to do so in sleep than in the waking consciousness. The immobility and semi-consciousness of the outer being during sleep enables the inner being to become "independent of the physical form, conscious in itself and master of its own life."[14] As Sri Aurobindo writes to a sadhak:

> You are more conscious in your sleep than in your waking condition. This is because of the physical consciousness which is not yet sufficiently open; it is only just beginning to open. In your sleep the inner being

---

13. Sri Aurobindo, *Letters on Yoga*, SABCL, Vol. 24, p. 1479.
14. The Mother, *Questions and Answers 1955*, CWM, Vol. 7, p. 70.

is active and the psychic there can influence more actively the mind and vital.[15]

It is because the inner being can be active more easily in sleep than in the waking state that spiritual experiences in yoga usually begin in sleep (and in indrawn meditation) rather than in the outer waking consciousness which does not give the inner being much chance to project itself into the waking state.[16]

The state of Samadhi or yogic trance, regarded in the traditional yogas as the culminating attainment of sadhana, is also more easily experienced in sleep in the form of *svapna-samādhi* or dream-trance. It is a state

> …in which one is conscious of inner experiences that are not dreams (i.e. the waking consciousness is lost for the time but it is replaced not by sleep but by an inward conscious state in which one moves in the supraphysical or the mental or vital being).[17]

As Sri Aurobindo writes:

> Many sadhaks here get at times or sometimes for a long period this deeper *svapna-samādhi* in what began as sleep — with the result that a conscious sadhana goes on in their sleeping as in their waking hours.[18]

15. Sri Aurobindo, *Letters on Yoga*, SABCL, Vol. 24, p. 1483.
16. Sri Aurobindo, *Letters on Yoga*, SABCL, Vol. 23, p. 883.
17. *Ibid.*, p. 1017.
18. *Ibid.*, p. 883.

To a sadhak who had an experience of *svapna-samādhi* and thought it was half-sleep, Sri Aurobindo wrote:

> It was not half sleep or quarter sleep or even one-sixteenth sleep that you had; it was a going inside of the consciousness, which in that state remains conscious but shut to outer things and open only to inner experience. You must distinguish clearly between these two quite different conditions, one is *nidrā*, the other, the beginning at least of *samādhi* (not *nirvikalpa*, of course!). This drawing inside is necessary because the active mind of the human being is at first too much turned to outward things; it has to go inside altogether in order to live in the inner being (inner mind, inner vital, inner physical, psychic). (p. 4)

To another disciple Sri Aurobindo similarly wrote:

> No, it was not sleep. You went inside into an inner consciousness; in this inner consciousness one is awake inside, but not outside, not conscious of external things but of inner things only. Your inner consciousness was busy doing what your outer mind had been trying to do, that is to work upon the thoughts and suggestions that bring restlessness and to put them right; it can be done much more easily by the inner consciousness than by the outer mind.[19]

19. Sri Aurobindo, *Letters on Yoga*, SABCL, Vol. 23, p. 1015.

The highest superconscient state of Sachchidananda, too, is more easily accessible in the state of Sushupti or sleep-trance than in the waking state. The Upanishadic description of the Superconscience, as the Sleep-Self, however, does not imply that everyone experiences Sachchidananda during sleep. This is made clear by the Mother's answer to a question:

> *The Upanishad says that when one sleeps, one reaches pure Being. Does this apply only to the Yogi or to everyone?*

> In theory, it applies to everyone. But the vast majority of human beings fall into unconsciousness, and if there is a contact with pure Being it is quite unconscious. Very few persons are conscious of this relation. It is usually the result of Yoga. (pp.17-18)

### Becoming Conscious in Sleep — Sadhana in Sleep

From the spiritual standpoint, our waking state is an unconscious slumber in which we are oblivious of the deeper subliminal depths and of the higher superconscient reaches of our being. The aim of sadhana is to wake up from our normal unconscious state which we euphemistically call the waking state in order to become conscious of our subliminal depths and superconscient heights. Sleep opens the door to these deeper and higher parts of our being and is thus potentially an aid in sadhana. However, ordinarily, con-

scious sadhana of the waking state is broken by the fall into
the semi-consciousness of sleep. There is not only an inter-
ruption of sadhana in ordinary sleep but also a temporary
loss of the good state of consciousness one has gained by
sadhana in the waking state. As Sri Aurobindo observes:

> The consciousness in the night almost always descends
> below the level of what one has gained by sadhana in
> the waking consciousness, unless there are special ex-
> periences of an uplifting character in the time of sleep
> or unless the yogic consciousness acquired is so strong
> in the physical itself as to counteract the pull of the
> subconscient inertia. (p. 63)

Hence the need to continue the sadhana in sleep and main-
tain the thread of progress by becoming more and more conscious in sleep. Doing so, says the Mother "has a double
effect: a negative effect, it prevents you from falling backward, losing whatever you have gained...and a positive effect, you make some progress...."[20]

The methods of sadhana by which the growth of consciousness takes place in the waking state also serve to make one
more and more conscious in sleep. However, Sri Aurobindo
and the Mother have recommended certain specific methods
for becoming more conscious in sleep. These consist in:

    1) Relaxing the body and putting the mind and vital to
    rest before falling asleep.

20. The Mother, *Words of the Mother*, CWM, Vol. 15, pp. 400-1.

2) Concentrating for a short time just before sleep, with the will or aspiration or prayer (depending on one's nature and inclination) to be conscious during sleep.

3) Passing into sleep in a state of concentration with the help of a mantra or some other means.

4) On waking up, remaining in a state of immobility for a while, without making an abrupt movement of the body, especially of the head, and concentrating to remember one's dream experiences.

5) Concentrating for a few minutes after rising in order to regain the true consciousness and get back the thread of progress.

The "night-school" of yoga for becoming conscious in sleep is an advanced school, where progress takes place only after sufficient gains have been made in sadhana during the waking state. As Sri Aurobindo states: "The sleep consciousness can be effectively dealt with only when the waking mind has made a certain amount of progress."(p. 65) and "It is usually only if there is much activity of sadhana in the day that it extends also into the sleep-state."(p. 65)

One should therefore bear in mind that becoming conscious in sleep so as to make sleep as much a part of sadhana as the waking state requires "always a settled endeavour and discipline and must take time, sometimes a long time. It will not do to refrain from effort because immediate results do not appear."(p. 63)

A.S. Dalal

# 1

## SLEEP — DOORWAY TO WORLDS WITHIN

...when you sleep you have one consciousness, and when you are awake you have another. In your waking state you look at things projected outside you, in your sleep state you see them interiorised. So it is as though in one case you were pushed altogether outside yourself, in front, and in the other it is as though you were looking at yourself in an inner mirror.[1]                                        — THE MOTHER

*

(Concerning unconsciousness during sleep) During sleep the inner beings become consciously active. When one wakes up, it is the waking being that is not conscious of the activities of the night.[2]                       — THE MOTHER

*

Sleep and waking are determined ... by the mind's waking condition or activity or its cessation — when it ceases for a time, then it is the subconscious that is there on the surface and there is sleep.[3]                          — SRI AUROBINDO

*

It is the waking mind which thinks and wills and controls more or less the life in the waking state. In the sleep that mind is not there and there is no control. It is not the think-ing mind that sees dreams etc. and is conscious in a rather incoherent way in sleep. It is usually what is called the subconscient that comes up then. If the waking mind were active in the body, one would not be able to sleep.[4]

SRI AUROBINDO

*

The outer consciousness goes down into this subconscient when we are asleep, and so it becomes unaware of what is going on in us when we are asleep except for a few dreams.[5]

SRI AUROBINDO

*

In the waking state it [the subconscient] is overpowered by the conscious thinking mind and vital and conscious physi-cal mind, but in the sleep state it comes on the surface.[6]

SRI AUROBINDO

*

*Does the subconscient go on recording during sleep?*

For most people, in their sleep, it is precisely what has been recorded in the subconscient during the day or previously which becomes active again and constitutes their dreams.[7]

THE MOTHER

*

When one is in the physical consciousness, then the sleep is apt to be of the subconscious kind, often heavy and unrefreshing, the dreams also of the subconscient kind, incoherent and meaningless or if there is a meaning the dream symbols are so confused and obscure that it is not possible to follow it.[8]          — SRI AUROBINDO

\*

The survival of the evil habits in sleep is easily explained and is a thing of common experience. It is a known psychological law that whatever is suppressed in the conscious mind remains in the subconscient being and recurs either in the waking state when the control is removed or else in sleep. Mental control by itself cannot eradicate anything entirely out of the being. The subconscient in the ordinary man includes the larger part of the vital being and the physical mind and also the secret body-consciousness. In order to make a true and complete change, one has to make all these conscious, to see clearly what is still there and to reject them from one layer after another till they have been entirely thrown out from the personal existence. Even then, they may remain and come back on the being from the surrounding universal forces and it is only when no part of the consciousness makes any response to these forces of the lower plane that the victory and transformation are absolutely complete.[9]

SRI AUROBINDO

\*

When the sleep is more awake, so to say, then one has

dreams of all kinds; when there is no such awareness of dreams, it is because the sleep of the body is more deep, — the dreams are there but the body consciousness does not note them or remember that it had them.[10]

SRI AUROBINDO

*

It was not half sleep or quarter sleep or even one-sixteenth sleep that you had; it was a going inside of the consciousness, which in that state remains conscious but shut to outer things and open only to inner experience. You must distinguish clearly between these two quite different conditions, one is *nidrā*[1], the other, the beginning at least of *samādhi*[2] (not *nirvikalpa*[3], of course!). This drawing inside is necessary because the active mind of the human being is at first too much turned to outward things; it has to go inside altogether in order to live in the inner being (inner mind, inner vital, inner physical, psychic). But with training one can arrive at a point when one remains outwardly conscious and yet lives in the inner being and has at will the indrawn or the outpoured condition; you can then have the same dense immobility and the same inpouring of a greater and purer con-

1 Sleep. (Ed.)

2 Yogic trance in which the mind acquires the capacity of withdrawing from its limited waking activities into freer and higher states of consciousness. (Ed.)

3 [Samadhi] in which there is no thought or movement of consciousness or awareness of other inner or outer things. (Ed.)

sciousness in the waking state as in that which you errone-
ously call sleep.[11]                              — SRI AUROBINDO

\*

The sleep you describe in which there is a luminous silence
or else the sleep in which there is Ananda in the cells, these
are obviously the best states. The other hours, those of which
you are unconscious, may be spells of a deep slumber in
which you have got out of the physical into the mental, vital
or other planes. You say you were unconscious, but it may
simply be that you do not remember what happened; for in
coming back there is a sort of turning over of the consciousness, a transition or reversal, in which everything experienced in sleep except perhaps the last happening of all or
else one that was very impressive, recedes from the physical
consciousness and all becomes as if a blank. There is another blank state, a state of inertia, not only blank, but heavy
and unremembering; but that is when one goes deeply and
crassly into the subconscient; this subterranean plunge is
very undesirable, obscuring, lowering, often fatiguing rather
than restful, the reverse of the luminous silence.[12]

                                              SRI AUROBINDO

\*

*Some people say that they have dreamless sleep for the
whole night. Is this possible?*

They simply mean that when they come back, they are not

conscious of having dreamed. In the sleep the consciousness goes into other planes and has experiences there and
when these are translated perfectly or imperfectly by the
physical mind, they are called dreams. All the time of sleep
such dreams take place, but sometimes one remembers and
at other times does not at all remember. Sometimes also one
goes low down into the subconscient and the dreams are
there, but so deep down that when one comes out there is
not even the consciousness that one had dreamed.[13]

SRI AUROBINDO

*

People's ideas of sound sleep are absolutely erroneous.
What they call sound sleep is merely a plunge of the outer
consciousness into a complete subconscience. They call that
a dreamless sleep; but it is only a state in which the surface
sleep consciousness which is a subtle prolongation of the
outer still left active in sleep itself is unable to record the
dreams and transmit them to the physical mind. As a matter
of fact the whole sleep is full of dreams. It is only during the
brief time in which one is in the Brahmaloka that the dreams
cease.[14]                                                  — SRI AUROBINDO

*

*What is the nature of dreamless sleep?*

Generally, when you have what you call dreamless sleep, it
is one of two things; either you do not remember what you

dreamt or you fell into absolute unconsciousness which is almost death — a taste of death. But there is the possibility of a sleep in which you enter into an absolute silence, immobility and peace in all parts of your being and your consciousness merges into Sachchidananda. You can hardly call it sleep, for it is extremely conscious. In that condition you may remain for a few minutes, but these few minutes give you more rest and refreshment than hours of ordinary sleep. You cannot have it by chance; it requires a long training.[15]

THE MOTHER

\*

*What is the nature of a sleep without dreams?*

If one succeeds in making the mind and vital silent, and in keeping the body well asleep, one can have a very still and quiet sleep, and then, if one can manage to get out of these forms and enter the higher worlds, one may reach the true repose of Sachchidananda.[16]            — THE MOTHER

\*

What happens in sleep is that our consciousness withdraws from the field of its waking experiences; it is supposed to be resting, suspended or in abeyance, but that is a superficial view of the matter. What is in abeyance is the waking activities, what is at rest is the surface mind and the normal conscious action of the bodily part of us; but the inner consciousness is not suspended, it enters into new inner activities, only a part of which, a part happening or recorded in something of us that is near to the surface, we remember. There is maintained in sleep, thus near the surface, an obscure subconscious element which is a receptacle or passage for our dream experiences and itself also a dream-builder; but behind it is the depth and mass of the subliminal, the totality of our concealed inner being and consciousness which is of quite another order. Normally it is a subconscient part in us, intermediate between consciousness and pure inconscience, that sends up through this surface layer its formations in the shape of dreams, constructions marked by an apparent inconsequence and incoherence. Many of these are fugitive structures built upon circumstances of our present life selected apparently at random and surrounded with a phantasy of variation; others call back the past, or rather selected circumstances and persons of the past, as a starting-point for similar fleeting edifices. There are other dreams of the subconscious which seem to be pure phantasy without any such initiation or basis....[17]

SRI AUROBINDO

*

Ordinarily when one sleeps a complex phenomenon happens. The waking consciousness is no longer there, for all has been withdrawn within into the inner realms of which we are not aware when we are awake, though they exist; for then all that is put behind a veil by the waking mind and nothing remains except the surface self and the outward world — much as the veil of the sunlight hides from us the vast worlds of the stars that are behind it. Sleep is a going inward in which the surface self and the outside world are put away from our sense and vision. But in ordinary sleep we do not become aware of the worlds within; the being seems submerged in a deep subconscience. On the surface of this subconscience floats an obscure layer in which dreams take place, as it seems to us, but, more correctly it may be said, are recorded. When we go very deeply asleep, we have what appears to us as a dreamless slumber; but, in fact, dreams are going on, but they are either too deep down to reach the recording surface or are forgotten, all recollection of their having existed even is wiped out in the transition to the waking consciousness. Ordinary dreams are for the most part or seem to be incoherent, because they are either woven by the subconscient out of deep-lying impressions left in it by our past inner and outer life, woven in a fantastic way which does not easily yield any clue of meaning to the waking mind's remembrance, or are fragmentary records, mostly distorted, of experiences which are going on behind the veil of sleep — very largely indeed these two elements get mixed up together. For, in fact, a large part of our consciousness in sleep does not get sunk into this subconscious state; it passes beyond the veil into other planes of being which are connected with our own inner planes, planes of supraphysical existence, worlds of a larger life, mind or psyche which are there behind and whose influences come to us without our knowledge. Occasionally we get a dream from these planes, something more than a dream, — a dream experience which is a record direct or symbolic of what happens to us or around us there. As the inner consciousness grows by sadhana, these dream experiences increase in number, clearness, coherence, accuracy and after some growth of experience and consciousness, we can, if we observe, come to understand them and their significance to our inner life. Even we can by training become so conscious as to follow our own passage, usually veiled to our awareness and memory, through many realms and the process of the return to the waking state. At a certain pitch of this inner wakefulness this kind of sleep, a sleep of experiences, can replace the ordinary subconscious slumber.

It is of course an inner being or consciousness or something of the inner self that grows in this way, not as usually it is, behind the veil of sleep, but in the sleep itself.[18]

SRI AUROBINDO

*

In the night the mental and vital, especially the vital are very active. During the day they are under check, the physical consciousnesss automatically represses their free play and expression. In sleep this check is removed and they come out with their natural and free movements.[19]

THE MOTHER

*

In sleep we leave the physical body, only a subconscient residue remaining, and enter all planes and all sorts of worlds. In each we see scenes, meet beings, share in happenings, come across formations, influences, suggestions which belong to these planes. Even when we are awake, part of us moves in these planes, but their activity goes on behind the veil; our waking minds are not aware of it.[20]

SRI AUROBINDO

\*

*I was sleeping but woke up exactly when it was time to attend classes. Was it the Divine who woke me up?*

Not necessarily. There is always a part of the subconscient which is awake, and it is sufficient to have the will to wake up at a certain hour to make this part awaken you.[21]

THE MOTHER

\*

Things happen there [on the vital plane] that have some connection with the nature and life here, but they happen differently because there it is not the physical beings that meet, but the vital beings of people. One can gather what is the nature of one's own inner vital being — which is often very different from the physical personality that acts in front in the body. By the acting of the consciousness in these dreams the inner parts of the being begin to be more active and have more influence on the outer nature.[22]    — SRI AUROBINDO

\*

*In vital nightmares, which part of the being goes out of the body?*

Your vital — not the whole of it for that would produce a cataleptic state, but a portion of the vital goes out for a stroll. Some always go to the nastiest places and so have very bad nights — the possibilities in these nightly rambles are innumerable. It may be a very small thing, just a little portion of your being, but if it is conscious, that is enough to give you a fine little nightmare!

You know, when you sleep, the inner beings are not concentrated upon the body, they go out and become more or less independent — a limited independence, but independence all the same — and they go to live in their own domains. The mind more so, for it is hardly held within the body, it is only concentrated but not contained in the body. The vital also goes beyond the body, but it is more concentrated upon the body.[23]                         — THE MOTHER

\*

*Please tell me what kind of tiring things I have been doing in my sleep.*

Bodily fatigue is a physical rendering of certain activities and contacts originating in the vital. In one's sleep one may go to evil places in the vital and meet evil beings.[24]

THE MOTHER

\*

*Why are the mind and vital so active at night? How could one control their activity at night?*

It is their function. So long as one is not perfectly conscious
in sleep, they will act.[25]                              — SRI AUROBINDO

                                          *

In the sleep part of the consciousness goes out to other
planes of being and sees and experiences things there. It is
quite possible for the witness consciousness to follow these
happenings which usually transmit themselves in a coherent transcription to the sleeping part of the consciousness
— the latter receives them and they appear as clear significant dreams as opposed to the incoherent dreams of the
subconscient. Or else the witness consciousness may feel
itself there watching the happenings as well as here.[26]

                                                    SRI AUROBINDO

                                          *

*At times when one goes out of the body, the body follows
the part which goes out.*

You are speaking of a somnambulist? But that is quite another thing. This means that the part which goes out (whether
a part of the mind or a part of the vital) is so strongly attached to the body, or rather that the body is so attached to
this part, that when this part decides to do something the
body follows it automatically. In your inner being you de-
cide to do a certain thing and your body is so closely tied to
your inner being that without thinking of it, without wanting
to do so, without making any effort, it follows and does the
same thing. Note that in this matter, the physical body has

capacities it would not have in the ordinary waking condition. For instance, it is well known that one can walk in dangerous places where one would find it rather difficult to walk in the waking state. The body follows the consciousness of the inner being and its own consciousness is asleep — for the body has a consciousness. All the parts of the being, including the most material, have an independent consciousness. Hence when you go to sleep dead tired, when your physical body needs rest absolutely, your physical consciousness sleeps, while the consciousness of your subtle physical body or your vital or of your mind does not sleep, it continues its activity; but your physical consciousness is separated from the body, it is asleep in a state of unconsciousness, and then the part which does not sleep, which is active, uses the body without the physical consciousness as intermediary and makes it do things directly. That is how one becomes a somnambulist. According to my experience, the waking consciousness goes to sleep for some reason or other (usually due to fatigue), but the inner being is awake, and the body is so tied to it that it follows it automatically. That is why you do fantastic things, because you do not see them physically, you see them in a different way.

> *It is said that somnambulism is due to serious pre-occupations and cares. Is this true? Tartini composed a sonata in this state, and when he got up in the morning, he wrote down the whole thing.*

Somnambulism is not always due to preoccupations and cares! Yes, there are people who write wonderful things when in a state of somnambulism. But Tartini was not a somnambulist — it was in the dream-state that he wrote sonatas.

The other state is always a little dangerous, always. Unexpected things can happen, an accident to the vital, for instance.

*How can one be cured of somnambulism?*

Quite simply, by putting a will upon the body before going to sleep. One becomes a somnambulist because the mind is not developed enough to break the inner ties. For the mind always separates the external being from the deeper consciousness. Little children are quite tied up. I knew children who were quite sincere but could not distinguish whether a thing was going on in their imagination or in reality. For them the inner life was as real as the external life. They were not telling stories, they were not liars; simply the inner life was as real as the external life. There are children who go night after night to the same spot in order to continue the dream they have begun — they are experts in the art of going out of their bodies.[27]                              — THE MOTHER

\*

*In the first and middle part of my sleep there is a great mental and vital activity but in the last part this activity subsides and I get various kinds of symbolic dreams and intimations of higher knowledge. What is the reason for this?*

In sleep one very commonly passes from consciousness to deeper consciousness in a long succession until one reaches the psychic and rests there or else from higher to higher consciousness until one reaches rest in some silence and peace. The few minutes one passes in this rest are the real sleep which restores, — if one does not get it, there is only a half rest. It is when you come near to either of these domains of rest that you begin to see these higher kinds of dreams.[28]

— SRI AUROBINDO

*

*What is the way to pass into the psychic or the higher consciousness in sleep and rest there?*

It is done unconsciously as it is. If one wants to do it consciously and regulate it, one has first to become conscious in sleep.[29]

— SRI AUROBINDO

*

A long unbroken sleep is necessary because there are just ten minutes of the whole into which one enters into a true rest — a sort of Sachchidananda immobility of consciousness — and that it is which really restores the system. The rest of the time is spent first in travelling through various states of consciousness towards that and then coming out of it back towards the waking state. This fact of the ten minutes true rest has been noted by medical men, but of course they know nothing about Sacchidananda.[30]

— SRI AUROBINDO

*

*Has the mind need of rest apart from the physical body and the physical brain?*

Yes, an absolute need. And it is only in silence that the mind can receive the true light from above. I do not think that the mental being is liable to fatigue; if it feels tired, that is rather a reaction of the brain. It is only in silence that it can rise above itself. But from the point of view of sleep and dreams of which we were speaking, there is a very remarkable phenomenon. I have tried it out. If you are able to establish not only silence in your head but also repose in your vital, the stoppage of all the activities of your being, and if coming out of the domain of forms you enter into what is called Sachchidananda, the supreme consciousness, then with three minutes of that state you can have more rest than in eight hours of sleep. It is not very easy, no…. It is the consciousness absolutely conscious but completely still, in the full original Light. If you get that, if you are able to immobilise everything in you, then your whole being participates in this supreme consciousness and I have well observed that as regards rest (and I mean by rest bodily rest, the repose of the muscles) three minutes of that state were equivalent to eight hours of ordinary sleep.[31]                      — THE MOTHER

*

*The Upanishad says that when one sleeps, one reaches pure Being. Does this apply only to the Yogi or to everyone?*

In theory, it applies to everyone. But the vast majority of human beings fall into unconsciousness, and if there is a contact with pure Being it is quite unconscious. Very few persons are conscious of this relation. It is usually the result of Yoga.[32]                                                    — THE MOTHER

*

Sleep like trance opens the gate of the subliminal to us; for in sleep, as in trance, we retire behind the veil of the limited waking personality and it is behind this veil that the sub-liminal has its existence. But we receive the records of our sleep experience through dream and in dream figures and not in that condition which might be called an inner waking and which is the most accessible form of the trance state, nor through the supernormal clarities of vision and other more luminous and concrete ways of communication devel-oped by the inner subliminal cognition when it gets into habitual or occasional conscious connection with our wak-ing self.[33]                                              — SRI AUROBINDO

*

When we sleep and the surface physical part of us, which is in its first origin here an output from the Inconscient, re-lapses towards the originating inconscience, it enters into this subconscious element, antechamber or substratum, and there it finds the impressions of its past or persistent habits of mind and experiences, — for all have left their mark on our subconscious part and have there a power of recurrence.

...In the dream-consciousness the phenomenon is an apparently fanciful construction, a composite of figures and movements built upon or around the buried impressions with a sense in them that escapes the waking intelligence because it has no clue to the subconscient's system of significances. After a time this subconscious activity appears to sink back into complete inconscience and we speak of this state as deep dreamless sleep; thence we emerge again into the dream-shallows or return to the waking surface.

But, in fact, in what we call dreamless sleep, we have gone into a profounder and denser layer of the subconscient, a state too involved, too immersed or too obscure, dull and heavy to bring to the surface its structures, and we are dreaming there but unable to grasp or retain in the recording layer of subconscience these more obscure dream-figures. Or else, it may be, the part of our mind which still remains active in the sleep of the body has entered into the inner domains of our being, the subliminal mental, the subliminal vital, the subtle-physical, and is there lost to all active connection with the surface parts of us. If we are still in the nearer depths of these regions, the surface subconscient which is our sleep-wakefulness records something of what we experience in these depths; but it records it in its own transcription, often marred by characteristic incoherences and always, even when most coherent, deformed or cast into figures drawn from the world of waking experience. But if we have gone deeper inward, the record fails or cannot be recovered and we have the illusion of dreamlessness; but the activity of the inner dream consciousness continues behind the veil of the now mute and inactive subconscient surface. This continued dream activity is revealed to us when we become more inwardly conscious, for then we get into connection with the heavier and deeper subconscient stratum and can be aware, — at the time or by a retracing or recovering through memory, — of what happened when we sank into these torpid depths. It is possible too to become conscious deeper within our subliminal selves and we are then aware of experiences on other planes of our being or even in supraphysical worlds to which sleep gives us a right of secret entry. A transcript of such experiences reaches us; but the transcriber here is not the subconscious, it is the subliminal, a greater dream-builder.

If the subliminal thus comes to the front in our dream-consciousness, there is sometimes an activity of our subliminal intelligence, — dream becomes a series of thoughts, often strangely or vividly figured, problems are solved which our waking consciousness could not solve, warnings, premonitions, indications of the future, veridical dreams replace the normal subconscious incoherence. There can come also a structure of symbol-images, some of a mental character, some of a vital nature: the former are precise in their figures, clear in their significance; the latter are often complex and baffling to our waking consciousness, but, if we can seize the clue, they reveal their own sense and peculiar system of coherence. Finally, there can come to us the records of happenings seen or experienced by us on other planes of our own being or of universal being into which we enter: these have sometimes, like the symbolic dreams, a strong bearing on our own inner and outer life or the life of others, reveal elements of our or their mental being and life-being or disclose influences on them of which our waking self is totally ignorant; but sometimes they have no such bearing and are purely records of other organised systems of consciousness independent of our physical existence. The subconscious dreams constitute the bulk of our most ordinary sleep-experience and they are those which we usually remember; but sometimes the subliminal builder is able to impress our sleep consciousness sufficiently to stamp his activities on our waking memory. If we develop our inner being, live more inwardly than most men do, then the balance is changed and a larger dream-consciousness opens before us; our dreams can take on a subliminal and no longer a subconscious character and can assume a reality and significance.

It is even possible to become wholly conscious in sleep and follow throughout from beginning to end or over large stretches the stages of our dream-experience; it is found that then we are aware of ourselves passing from state after state of consciousness to a brief period of luminous and peaceful dreamless rest, which is the true restorer of the energies of the waking nature, and then returning by the same way to the waking consciousness. It is normal, as we thus pass from state to state, to let the previous experiences slip away from us; in the return only the more vivid or those nearest to the waking surface are remembered: but this can be remedied, — a greater retention is possible or the power can be developed of going back in memory from dream to dream, from state to state, till the whole is once more before us. A coherent knowledge of sleep-life, though difficult to achieve or to keep established, is possible.[34]                    — SRI AUROBINDO

# 2

## DREAMS AND DREAM-EXPERIENCES

It is the subconscient that is active in the ordinary dreams. But in the dreams in which one goes out into other planes of consciousness, mental, vital, subtle physical, it is part of the inner being, inner mental or vital or physical that is usually active.[35] — SRI AUROBINDO

*

Dreams are often only incoherent constructions of our subconscient, but others are records (often much mixed and distorted) or transcripts of experiences in these supra-physical planes. When we do sadhana, this kind of dream becomes very common; then subconscious dreams cease to predominate.[36] — SRI AUROBINDO

*

...the dreams of most people are recorded by the subconscient. Either the whole thing is a creation of the subconscient and turns out, if recorded, to be incoherent and lacking in any sense, or, if there is a real communication from a higher plane, marked by a sense of elevation and wonder, it gets transcribed by the subconscient and what that forms is either flat or ludicrous.[37] — SRI AUROBINDO

*

Many of these dreams rise up from the subconscient and are made up of old memories, impressions etc. put together in an incoherent way. For the subconscient receives impressions of all we do or experience in our lives and keeps these impressions in it, sending up often fragments of them in sleep.[38]      — SRI AUROBINDO

\*

It often happens that when something is thrown out of the waking consciousness it still occurs in dream. This recurrence is of two kinds. One is when the thing is gone, but the memory and impression of it remains in the subconscient and comes up in dream form in sleep. These subconscient dream-recurrences are of no importance; they are shadows rather than realities. The other is when dreams come in the vital to test or to show how far in some part of the inner being the old movement remains or is conquered. For in sleep the control of the waking consciousness and will is not there. If then even in spite of that one is conscious in sleep and either does not feel the old movement when the circumstances that formerly caused it are repeated in dream or else soon conquers and throws it out, then it must be understood that there too the victory is won.[39]

SRI AUROBINDO

\*

The physical mind (or else the subconscient) almost always interferes in the dream and gives its own version. It is only

when there is a clear experience on the mental or vital plane
that it does not try to interfere.[40]        — SRI AUROBINDO

\*

It is only the subconscious belt that is chaotic in its dream
sequences; for its transcriptions are fantastic and often
mixed, combining a jumble of different elements: some play
with impressions from the past, some translate outward
touches pressing on the sleep-mind; most are fragments
from successive dream experiences that are not really part
of one connected experience — as if a gramophone record
were to be made up of snatches of different songs all jum-
bled together. The vital dreams even in the subconscious
range are often coherent in themselves and only seem incoherent to the waking intelligence because the logic and law
of their sequences is different from the logic and law which
the physical reason imposes on the incoherences of physical life. But if one gets the guiding clue and if one has some
dream-experience and dream-insight, then it is possible to
seize the links of the sequences and make out the significance, often very profound or very striking, both of the detail and of the whole. Deeper in, we come to perfectly
coherent dreams recording the experience of the inner vital
and inner mental planes; there are also true psychic dreams
— the latter usually are of a great beauty. Some of these
mental or vital plane dream-experiences, however, are symbolic, very many in fact, and can only be understood if one
is familiar with or gets the clue to the symbols.[41]

SRI AUROBINDO

\*

Dreams of this kind [subconscient] can last for years and years after the waking consciousness has ceased to interest itself in things of that kind. The subconscient is exceedingly obstinate in the keeping of its old impressions. I find myself even recently having a dream of revolutionary activities or another in which the Maharaja of Baroda butted in, people and things I have not even thought of passingly for the last twenty years almost. I suppose it is because the very business of the subconscient in the human psychology is to keep all the past inside it and, being without conscious mentality, it clings to its office until the light has fully come down into it, illumining even its corners and crevices.[42]

SRI AUROBINDO

\*

In dream it is usually the case that even what one has thrown out from the waking state, comes up for a long time — that is because all these things remain still in the subconscient and it is the subconscient that creates a great part of people's dreams. Thus if one no longer has sexual desires in the waking state he can still have sex-dreams — and emissions — with a more or less frequent recurrence; he can still meet people in dreams whom he never sees or hears or thinks of in his waking hours — and so on. All the more are such dreams likely to come when the waking mind is not free.[43]

SRI AUROBINDO

\*

Dreams of this kind arise from the subconscient. It is one of the most embarrassing elements of yogic experience to find

how obstinately the subconscient retains what has been settled and done with in the upper layers of the consciousness.
But just for that reason these dreams are often a useful indication as they enable us to pursue things to their obscure
roots in this underworld and excise them.[44]

SRI AUROBINDO

*

I said this dream was an actual happening on the vital plane,
not a formation. If somebody attacks you in the street, that
is not a formation. But if somebody hypnotises you and suggests that you are ill — that suggestion is a formation put in
by the hypnotiser.[45]

SRI AUROBINDO

*

These dreams are not all mere dreams, all have not a casual,
incoherent or subconscious building. Many are records or
transcripts of experiences on the vital plane into which one
enters in sleep, some are scenes or events of the subtle physical plane. There one often undergoes happenings or carries
on actions that resemble those of the physical life with the
same surroundings and the same people, though usually
there is in arrangement and feature some or a considerable
difference. But it may also be a contact with other surroundings and with other people, not known in the physical life or
not belonging at all to the physical world.[46]

SRI AUROBINDO

*

...there is an experience, a fact, something happens — there is also its translation in your brain. When you wake up it is a sort of interpretation of your dream which you remember. It is very rarely that one is conscious at the time the experience occurs and conscious of the experience as it really is. For that one must be very wakeful during the night, quite awake in one's sleep. Usually this is not the case. There is one part of the being which has an experience; when that part of the being which had gone out of the body re-enters it, it brings back the experience, the brain receives a contact with this experience, translates it by images, words, ideas, impressions, feelings, and when one wakes up one catches something of this, and with that makes a "dream". But it is only a transcription of something that has happened — which has an analogy, a similarity, but which wasn't exactly what one receives as a dream.[47] — THE MOTHER

*

*How can one distinguish a dream from an experience?*

In a general way, a dream leaves a confused and fleeting impression, whereas an experience awakens a deep and lasting feeling.

But the shades of difference are subtle and many, and it is by a very attentive and sincere observation (that is to say, free from bias and preference) that one gradually learns to discern the one from the other.[48] — THE MOTHER

*

All dreams of this kind are very obviously formations such as one often meets on the vital, more rarely on the mental plane. Sometimes they are the formations of your own mind or vital; sometimes they are the formations of other minds with an exact or modified transcription in yours; sometimes formations come that are made by the non-human forces or beings of these other planes. These things are not true and need not become true in the physical world, but they may still have effects on the physical if they are framed with that purpose or that tendency and, if they are allowed, they may realise their events or their meaning — for they are most often symbolical or schematic — in the inner or the outer life. The proper course with them is simply to observe and understand and, if they are from a hostile source, reject or destroy them.

There are other dreams that have not the same character but are a representation or transcription of things that actually happen on other planes, in other worlds under other conditions than ours. There are, again, some dreams that are purely symbolic and some that indicate existing movements and propensities in us, whether familiar or undetected by the waking mind, or exploit old memories or else raise up things either passively stored or still active in the subconscient, a mass of various stuff which has to be changed or got rid of as one rises into a higher consciousness. If one learns how to interpret, one can get from dreams much knowledge of the secrets of our nature and of other-nature.[49]

SRI AUROBINDO

*

On the mental plane all the formations made by the mind — the actual "forms" that it gives to the thoughts — return and appear to you as if they were coming from outside and give you dreams. Most dreams are like that. Some people have a very conscious mental life and are able to enter the mental plane and move about in it with the same independence they have in physical life; these people have mentally objective nights. But most people are incapable of doing this: it is their mental activity going on during sleep and assuming forms, and these forms give them what they call dreams.

There is a very common example — it is amusing because it is rather vivid. If you have quarrelled with someone during the day, you may wish to hit him, to say very unpleasant things to him. You control yourself, you don't do it, but your thought, your mind is at work and in your sleep you suddenly have a terrible dream. Someone approaches you with a stick and you hit each other and have a real fight. And when you wake up, if you don't know, if you don't understand what has happened, you say to yourself, "What an unpleasant dream I had!" But in fact it is your own thought which came back to you, like that.

So be on your guard when you dream that someone is unkind to you! First of all, you should ask yourself, "But didn't I have a bad thought against him?".[50]

THE MOTHER

*

It is a very small number of dreams that can be so explained [that they arise by external stimuli] and in many cases the explanation is quite arbitrary or cannot be proved. A much larger number of dreams arise from subconscient impressions of the past without any stimulus from outside. These are the dreams from the subconscient which are the bulk of those remembered by people who live in the external mind mostly. There are also the dreams that are renderings of vital movements and tendencies habitual to the nature, personal formations of the vital plane. But when one begins to live within then the dreams are often transcriptions of one's experiences on the vital plane and beyond that there is a large field of symbolic and other dreams which have nothing to do with memory.[51]      — SRI AUROBINDO

*

*In the invisible worlds, are things seen as in the physical world or as in dreams?*

We have to agree on what dreams are! There are dreams where you see things so precisely, so concretely that the material world seems rather unreal in comparison. There are dreams like that where things are so intense, so precise, so concrete, so objective and leave you with such a vivid impression that the material world seems rather misty, not very clear, not very distinct. So, if it is a dream like that, yes. But if it is a dream where things clash incoherently, inconsistently with one another, no.[52]      — THE MOTHER

*

[Regarding a bad dream] I call that mental fermentation. As soon as your waking consciousness falls asleep or leaves your body, the brain-cells you have not taken the trouble to quiet down begin to fidget restlessly and produce what is called a dream, but it is nothing more than disorderly activity. It has no meaning and can serve only one purpose: to make you aware of what goes on in your head.[53]

THE MOTHER

*

... nightmares? These are your sorties into the vital world. And what is the first thing you try to do when you are in the grip of a nightmare? You rush back into your body and shake yourself into your normal physical consciousness. But in the world of the vital forces you are a stranger; it is an uncharted sea in which you have neither compass nor rudder. You do not know how to go, you do not know where to go and at each step you do just the opposite of what should be done. Directly you enter any realm of this world, its beings gather round you and want to encompass and get out of you all you have, to draw what they can and make it a food and a prey. If you have no strong light and force radiating from within you, you move there without your body as if you had no coat to protect you against a chill and bleak atmosphere, no house to shield you, even no skin covering you, your nerves exposed and bare.[54]

— THE MOTHER

*

Nightmares like X's are contacts with this side of the vital plane. Its influences are also the source of much in men that is demoniac, dirty, cruel and base.[55]          — SRI AUROBINDO

*

*During sleep I often get bad dreams of the vital plane. How to prevent this?*

You can do it by having a will in the waking state against these things coming in the dream, before you go to sleep for instance. It will not succeed at once but it will in the end. Or else you must aspire to grow more conscious in sleep.[56]

SRI AUROBINDO

*

*When we sleep, our consciousness goes out, doesn't it? But other people have dreams in which I appear. So what happens? Does the consciousness divide itself or are other people's dreams only their own imagination?*

Most often, it is the vital consciousness that goes out of the body and has the form, the appearance of the person's body. If one person dreams of another, it means that both have met at night, most often in the vital region, but it can also happen elsewhere, in the subtle physical or the mental. There are any number of different possibilities in dreams.[57]

THE MOTHER

*

When one dreams, one goes very often into his subliminal

being, and there things are almost the same and yet not absolutely the same; there is a great resemblance and yet there is a difference; and usually this is greater. One has the impression of entering into something that's vaster; and, for example, one feels that one can do more, that one knows more, one has a power and clear-sightedness which one doesn't have in the ordinary consciousness; one has the impression while dreaming that one knows many more things than when one is awake. No? Doesn't this happen? You don't have dreams like that?... when one dreams and knows a lot, for example, about the secret causes of things, about what a movement expresses... all that, one feels that one knows it. For instance, when one dreams of someone, one knows better what he thinks, what he wants, all these things, better than when one is in waking contact with him. This happens when one has entered the subliminal. Very often one dreams in the subliminal.[58]                 — THE MOTHER

*

...symbolic dreams are usually very coherent, one remembers everything, to the least detail; it is more living, more real, more intense than the material life, and it is fairly rare. When one returns from a symbolic dream, one remembers everything, all the details, and feels that one has lived for those moments a much intenser and truer life than the physical one. And it leaves a very deep impression upon you. This does not happen very often, you know. Usually it comes when it is very necessary.[59]                 — THE MOTHER

*

There is no solid connection [between the waking and the dream states], but there can be a subtle one. Events of the waking state often influence the dream world, provided they have a sufficient repercussion on the mind or the vital. Formations and activities of the dream planes can project something of themselves or of their influence into the waking physical state, though they seldom reproduce themselves with any exactness there. It is only if the dream consciousness is very highly developed that one can usually see things there that are afterwards confirmed by thoughts, speech or actions of people or events in the physical world.[60]

SRI AUROBINDO

*

This is an instance of a dream of exact physical prevision. The power to have such dreams is comparatively rare, for ordinarily such previsions come in inner vision but not in sleep. In dreams vital or mental formations often take shape which sometimes fulfil themselves in essence, but not with this accuracy of detail.

It is only a particular class of dreams that do that [indicate the exact past and the future]. Most coherent dreams are either symbolic or indicate things that take place in the mental or vital planes rather than on the physical.[61]

SRI AUROBINDO

*

There are all kinds of premonitory dreams. There are premonitory dreams that are fulfilled immediately, that is to say, you dream in the night what will happen on the next day, and there are premonitory dreams that are fulfilled over varying lengths of time. And according to their position in time, these dreams are seen on various planes.

The higher we rise towards absolute certainty, the greater the distance is, because these visions belong to a region which is very close to the Origin and the length of time between the revelation of what is going to be and its realisation may be very great. But the revelation is certain, because it is very close to the Origin. There is a place — when one is identified with the Supreme — where one knows everything absolutely, in the past, the present, the future and everywhere. But usually people who go there forget what they have seen when they return. An extremely strict discipline is needed to remember. And that is the only place where one cannot make a mistake.

But the links of the chain of communication are not always all there and one very rarely remembers.[62]

THE MOTHER

*

*Sweet Mother, what is the difference between a symbolic dream and a vision?*

Usually one has a vision when one is not asleep, when one is awake. When one is awake and enters within oneself — whether in meditation or concentration — one has visions. Or at night you can't sleep... remain stretched out, remain quiet, don't sleep and you may have visions.

Dreams come when one is asleep, that is, when one has no longer the waking consciousness; whereas in vision one is in the waking consciousness, but one quietens or immobilises it, and it is another more inner consciousness which awakens; yet one is not asleep, the body is not asleep, it is just made quiet.

One can have visions even while remaining active. Some people have visions even amidst activity. Vision is another plane of perception which awakes. It is the senses in the mind or vital or physical which wake up and manage to pass their experiences to the outer consciousness. It is as though one had another pair of eyes behind these, eyes which could see in the vital instead of seeing in the physical. And this is always there. Only, as one is concentrated on the most material life, one doesn't notice it. But some children have the two conjointly, they see even physically all kinds of things which are not physical. Usually they are told that they are saying stupid things; so they stop speaking about them. But they don't see just this, only physically, they see other things behind. One can have visions with closed eyes, one can have visions with open eyes; while when dreaming one is always asleep.[63]                            — THE MOTHER

\*

...very rarely do dreams consist of true memories of past lives, because for that one must dream in one's psychic consciousness and there are not many who are capable of this. One dreams in the mental or vital consciousness but rarely does one dream in the psychic consciousness. That can happen, but it is rare.[64]                                    — THE MOTHER

*

Very few dreams have a meaning, an instructive value, but all dreams can show you what your present state of consciousness is and how things are combined in the subconscious, what the terrestrial influences are, what traces they leave and how they are combined. This is a very interesting subject of study.[65]                              — THE MOTHER

# 3

# REMEMBERING AND UNDERSTANDING DREAMS

The subconscient [during sleep] remains in the body. The being really goes out into different planes of consciousness, but its experiences are not kept in the memory, because the recording consciousness is too submerged to carry the record to the waking mind.[66] — SRI AUROBINDO

*

*Why do we forget our dreams?*

Because you do not dream always at the same place. It is not always the same part of your being that dreams and it is not at the same place that you dream. If you were in conscious, direct, continuous communication with all the parts of your being, you would remember all your dreams. But very few parts of the being are in communication.

For example, you have a dream in the subtle physical, that is to say, quite close to the physical. Generally, these dreams occur in the early hours of the morning, that is between four and five o'clock, at the end of the sleep. If you do not make a sudden movement when you wake up, if you remain very quiet, very still and a little attentive — quietly attentive — and concentrated, you will remember them, for the communication between the subtle physical and the physical is established — very rarely is there no communication.

Now, dreams are mostly forgotten because you have a dream while in a certain state and then pass into another. For instance, when you sleep, your body is asleep, your vital is asleep, but your mind is still active. So your mind begins to have dreams, that is, its activity is more or less coordinated, the imagination is very active and you see all kinds of things, take part in extraordinary happenings.... After some time, all that calms down and the mind also begins to doze. The vital that was resting wakes up; it comes out of the body, walks about, goes here and there, does all kinds of things, reacts, sometimes fights, and finally eats. It does all kinds of things. The vital is very adventurous. It watches. When it is heroic it rushes to save people who are in prison or to destroy enemies or it makes wonderful discoveries. But this pushes back the whole mental dream very far behind. It is rubbed off, forgotten: naturally you cannot remember it because the vital dream takes its place. But if you wake up suddenly at that moment, you remember it. There are people who have made the experiment, who have got up at certain fixed hours of the night and when they wake up suddenly, they do remember. You must not move brusquely, but awake in the natural course, then you remember.

After a time, the vital having taken a good stroll, needs to rest also, and so it goes into repose and quietness, quite tired at the end of all kinds of adventures. Then something else wakes up. Let us suppose that it is the subtle physical that goes for a walk. It starts moving and begins wandering, seeing the rooms and... why, this thing that was there, but it has come here and that other thing which was in that room is now in this one, and so on. If you wake up without stirring, you remember. But this has pushed away far to the back of the consciousness all the stories of the vital. They are forgotten and so you cannot recollect your dreams. But if at the time of waking up you are not in a hurry, you are not obliged to leave your bed, on the contrary you can remain there as long as you wish, you need not even open your eyes; you keep your head exactly where it was and you make yourself like a tranquil mirror within and concentrate there. You catch just a tiny end of the tail of your dream. You catch it and start pulling gently, without stirring in the least. You begin pulling quite gently, and then first one part comes, a little later another. You go backward; the last comes up first. Everything goes backward, slowly, and suddenly the whole dream reappears: "Ah, there! it was like that." Above all, do not jump up, do not stir; you repeat the dream to yourself several times — once, twice — until it becomes clear in all its details. Once that dream is settled, you continue not to stir, you try to go further in, and suddenly you catch the tail of something else. It is more distant, more vague, but you can still seize it. And here also you hang on, get hold of it and pull, and you see that everything changes and you enter another world; all of a sudden you have an extraordinary adventure — it is another dream. You follow the same process. You repeat the dream to yourself once, twice, until you are sure of it. You remain very quiet all the time. Then you begin to penetrate still more deeply into yourself, as though you were going in very far, very far; and again suddenly you see a vague form, you have a feeling, a sensation... like a current of air, a slight breeze, a little breath; and you say, "Well, well...." It takes a form, it becomes clear — and the third category comes. You must have a lot of time, a lot of patience, you must be very quiet in your mind and body, very quiet, and you can tell the story of your whole night from the end right up to the beginning.

Even without doing this exercise which is very long and difficult, in order to recollect a dream, whether it be the last one or the one in the middle that has made a violent impression on your being, you must do what I have said when you wake up: take particular care not even to move your head on the pillow, remain absolutely still and let the dream return.

Some people do not have a passage between one state and another, there is a little gap and so they leap from one to the other; there is no highway passing through all the states of being with no break of the consciousness. A small dark hole, and you do not remember. It is like a precipice across which one has to extend the consciousness. To build a bridge takes a very long time; it takes much longer than building a physical bridge.... Very few people want to and know how to do it. They may have had magnificent activities, they do not remember them or sometimes only the last, the nearest, the most physical activity, with an uncoordinated movement — dreams having no sense.[67]                    — THE MOTHER

*

It depends on the connection between the two states of consciousness at the time of waking. Usually there is a turn over of the consciousness in which the dream-state disappears more or less abruptly, effacing the fugitive impression made by the dream events (or rather their transcription) on the physical sheath. If the waking is more composed (less abrupt) or, if the impression is very strong, then the memory remains at least of the last dream. In the last case one may remember the dream for a long time, but usually after getting up the dream memories fade away. Those who want to remember their dreams sometimes make a practice of lying quiet and tracing backwards, recovering the dreams one by one. When the dream-state is very light, one can remember more dreams than when it is heavy.[68]          — SRI AUROBINDO

*

Most people move most in the vital in sleep because it is the nearest to the physical and easiest to remain. One does enter the higher planes but either the transit there is brief or one does not remember. For in returning to the waking consciousness it is again through the lower vital and subtle physical that one passes and as these are the last dreams they are more easily remembered. The other dreams are remembered only if (1) they are strongly impressed on the recording consciousness, (2) one wakes immediately after one of them, (3) one has learned to be conscious in sleep, i.e. follows consciously the passage from plane to plane. Some train themselves to remember by remaining without moving when they wake and following back the thread of the dreams.[69]          — SRI AUROBINDO

*

Yes, certainly, dream experiences can have a great value in

them and convey truths that are not so easy to get in the waking state.

It often happens like that. There is a change or reversal of the consciousness that takes place and the dream consciousness in disappearing takes away its scenes and experiences with it. This can sometimes be avoided by not coming out abruptly into the waking state or getting up quickly, but remaining quiet for a time to see if the memory remains or comes back. Otherwise the physical memory has to be taught to remember.[70]                    — SRI AUROBINDO

\*

*Is it not also necessary to remember one's dreams?*

This is not so necessary. It is useful if one wants to have a great control over his sleep. But this also one must know how to do. To remember one's dreams.... In the morning when you get up, you must not be in a hurry. That is, you must not wake up just at the moment when you must get out of bed; you must have some time in hand and must take good care, must make a formation before going to sleep, and take good care when waking up not to make any abrupt movement, because if you make an abrupt movement, automatically the memory of your dreams vanishes.[71]

THE MOTHER

\*

*Have dreams any significance? Is there any meaning*

*in the dreams of the subconscient?*

A dream, when it is not from the subconscient, is either symbolic or else an experience of some supraphysical plane or a formation therein by some mental or vital or other force or in rare cases an indication of some event actual or probable in the past, present or future. A dream from the subconscious plane has no meaning; it is simply a *kichadi** of impressions and memories left in the subconscient from the past.[72]

SRI AUROBINDO

*

Usually I give no "meaning" to dreams, because each one has his own symbolism which has a meaning only for himself.[73]          — THE MOTHER

*

*Sometimes in dreams one goes into houses, streets, places one has never seen. What does this mean?*

There may be many reasons for this. Perhaps it is an exteriorisation: one has come out of the body and gone for a stroll. They may be memories of former lives. Perhaps one has become identified with someone else's consciousness and has the memories of this other person. Perhaps it is a premonition (this is the rarest case, but it may happen): one

---

* hotch-potch (Ed.)

sees ahead what one will see later.

The other day I spoke to you about those landscapes of Japan; well, almost all — the most beautiful, the most striking ones — I had seen in vision in France; and yet I had not seen any pictures or photographs of Japan, I knew nothing of Japan. And I had seen these landscapes without human beings, nothing but the landscape, quite pure, like that, and it had seemed to me they were visions of a world other than the physical; they seemed to me too beautiful for the physical world, too perfectly beautiful. Particularly I used to see very often those stairs rising straight up into the sky; in my vision there was the impression of climbing straight up, straight up, and as though one could go on climbing, climbing, climbing. ... It had struck me, and the first time I saw this in Nature down there, I understood that I had already seen it in France before having known anything about Japan.

There are always many explanations possible and it is very difficult to explain for someone else. For oneself, if one has studied very carefully one's dreams and activities of the night, one can distinguish fine nuances. I was saying I thought I had a vision of another world — I knew it was something which existed, but I could not imagine there was a country where it existed; this seemed to me impossible, so very beautiful it was. It was the active mind which interfered. But I knew that what I was seeing truly existed, and it was only when I saw these landscapes physically that I realised in fact that I had seen something which existed, but I had seen it with inner eyes (it was the subtle-physical) before seeing it physically. Everyone has certain very small indications, but for that one must be very, very methodical, very scrupulous,

very careful in one's observation and not neglect the least
signs, and above all not give favourable mental explanations
to the experiences one has. For if one wants to explain to
oneself (I don't even speak of explaining to others), if one
wants to explain the experience to oneself advantageously,
to draw satisfaction, one does not understand anything any
more. That is, one may mix up the signs without even notic-
ing that they are mixed up. For instance, when one sees somebody in a dream (I am not speaking of dreams in which you
see somebody unknown, but of those where you see somebody you know, who comes to see you) there are all sorts of
explanations possible. If it is someone living far away from
you, in another country, perhaps that person has written a
letter to you and the letter is on the way, so you see this
person because he has put a formation of himself in his letter, a concentration; you see the person and the next morning
you get the letter. This is a very frequent occurrence. If it is a
person with a very strong thought-power, he may think of
you from very far, from his own country and concentrate his
thought, and this concentration takes the form of that person
in your consciousness. Perhaps it is that this person is calling
you intentionally; deliberately he comes to tell you something or give you a sign, if he is in danger, if he is sick. Suppose he has something important to tell you, he begins to
concentrate (he knows how to do it, as everyone does not)
and he enters your atmosphere, comes to tell you something
special. Now if you are passive and attentive, you receive the
message. And then, two more instances still: someone has
exteriorised himself more or less materially in his sleep and
has come to see you. And you become conscious of this

person because (almost by miracle) you are in a corresponding state of consciousness. And finally, a last instance, this
person may be dead and may come to see you after his death
(one part of him or almost the whole of his being according
to the relation you have with him). Consequently, for someone who is not very, very careful it is very difficult to distinguish these nuances, very difficult. On the other hand, quite
often imaginative people will tell you, "Oh! I saw this person — he is dead.'' I have heard that I don't know how many
times. These are people whose imagination runs freely. It is
possible that the person is dead, but not because he has appeared to you! ... One must pay great attention to the outer
forms things take. There are shades very difficult to distinguish, one must be very, very careful. For oneself, if one is in
the habit of studying all this, one can become aware of the
differences, but to interpret another's experiences is very difficult, unless he gives you in great detail all that surrounds
the dream, the vision: the ideas he had before, the ideas he
had later, the state of his health, the feelings he experienced
when going to sleep, the activities of the preceding day, indeed, all sorts of things. People who tell you, "Oh! I had this
vision, explain it to me!", that is childishness — unless it is
someone whom you have followed very carefully, whom you
yourself have taught how to recognise the planes, and whose
habits, whose reactions you know; otherwise it is impossible
to explain, for there are innumerable explanations for one
single thing.[74]        — THE MOTHER

\*

*How is it that the symbolism of dreams varies according to traditions, races, religions?*

Because the form given to the dream is mental. If you have learnt that such and such a form represents such and such a mythological person, you see that form and say: "It is that." In your mind there is an association between certain ideas and certain forms, and this is continued in the dream. When you translate your dream you give it an explanation corresponding to what you have learnt, what you have been taught, and it is with the mental image you have in your head that you know. Moreover, I have explained this to you a little later in the vision of Joan of Arc (Mother takes her book and reads):

"The beings who were always appearing and speaking to Jeanne d'Arc would, if seen by an Indian, have quite a different appearance; for when one sees, one projects the forms of one's mind…. You have the vision of one in India whom you call the Divine Mother; the Catholics say it is the Virgin Mary, and the Japanese call it Kwannon, the Goddess of Mercy; and others would give other names. It is the same force, the same power, but the images made of it are different in different faiths."[75]

— THE MOTHER

*

The people of dream are very often different from the people of actuality. Sometimes it is the real man who comes on another plane — sometimes it is a thought, force etc. that put on his appearance by some trick of association or other reason.[76] — SRI AUROBINDO

\*

[In dreams] the figures of the physical mother and father and relatives are very often symbolical of the physical or the hereditary nature or generally of the ordinary nature in which we are born.[77] — SRI AUROBINDO

\*

In these dreams the parents or relatives mean the ordinary forces of the physical consciousness (the old nature).[78]

SRI AUROBINDO

\*

*How is it that one meets and recognises in dream persons whom one is going to meet and recognise later on in ordinary life?*

There are many possibilities. But most often, it is that a communication has been established either on the mental or the vital plane or even on the subtle physical plane and it is this communication which brings about the meeting later — your dream is not only a premonition but also a condition; there is an inner relation close enough to enable you to come into contact in sleep, and circumstances so arrange themselves that you meet physically afterwards. Sometimes it is

only a premonition, but then the dream has a special quality
— you see someone coming and he does come physically a
little later.

Generally it is an already established relation; it is someone whom you meet, whom you frequent, whom you speak
to, with whom you live some hours of the night. Then afterwards when you both meet you have the impression that you
know each other very well. That's a fact, you already know
each other, before having met physically.[79]   — The Mother

*

> *Mother, at night if one sees someone dying, and a few
> months later one sees again the same person dying,
> what does it mean? Is this person in danger?*

In a dream, one sees a person... and a few months later one
sees him again?...

> *Yes, dying.*

One sees a person dying and then some months later one
sees him dying a second time, the same person! He is dead
or alive?

> *Alive.*

This is becoming disquieting, my child! I don't know; it
depends absolutely upon the case.

It can be a spiritual death, it can be a vital death, it can be the death of something in the being which ought to disappear (and then it means a progress), it can be a premonition, it can be lots of things. Unless you have the context of your dream one can't explain it. But you should have what we could call a jurisprudence of your dreams. You have never compared the dream with the events which occur?... for example, hasn't it happened to you — I know it has — that you see someone dying and this person really dies? But you don't see him dying again a second time. If you see the same dream twice, it means one of two things: either that he has lost once more another state of being, you see, that he has entered a vital consciousness or later from this vital consciousness he has gone out to enter a psychic consciousness. It can be that. But then there are sure signs. The dream cannot deceive you, and it cannot be similar. Or it may be simply that there was something which was profoundly impressed in the thought, in the brain, and that in certain circumstances which can have many causes... yet in certain circumstances... this impression begins to be active again and gives you the same dream once more. If it is an identical dream, it can be this, just a cerebral phenomenon.

Many dreams are just phenomena of the brain, that is, of things which go into activity again under some stimulus or other and bring back the same pictures, sometimes exactly the same, sometimes with slightly different associations and connections; so there are differences.

At times some dreams are repeated, you know, often dreams which are lessons or indications, dreams which announce something to you or want to draw your attention to something or put you on your guard against something. Very often it happens that they recur either at brief intervals or at a certain distance. And usually it means that the first time the impression was very faint, one doesn't remember it well. The third time or even after the second, one has a vague impression already: "Why! This isn't the first time", when one sees it. Then the third time it is clear, precise, absolute, and one remembers: "Ah, I have already seen this thrice!"

Usually these dreams are extremely interesting and give you precise indications: either about something to be done or something not to be done, or about precautions to be taken or perhaps about your relations with someone, what you should expect to receive from a person, how you should act towards him or in certain circumstances.

You see it is quite a small detail, a very small detail which recurs in this way; sometimes it comes immediately: one night, the second night, the third night; sometimes it takes weeks to recur.[80]                                  — THE MOTHER

*

These are dreams of the vital plane — they have probably some reference to something going on in your vital, but these dreams cannot be precisely interpreted unless there is either a clue that is clear on the surface or else you yourself can relate it to something in your experience of which you are aware. The images of the ascent and the coming down of water (consciousness or some other gift from above) are frequent and the general meaning is always the same — but the precise significance here is not clear.[81]     — SRI AUROBINDO

*

A great many people have these dreams. It is the vital being that goes out in sleep and moves about in the vital worlds and has this sense of floating in the air in its own (vital) body. The waves of a sea having the colour of lightning must have been the atmosphere of some vital province. I have known of some sadhaks, when they go at first out of the body in a more conscious way, thinking they have actually levitated, the vividness of the movement is so intense, but it is simply the vital body going out.[82]

SRI AUROBINDO

*

The experience of being taken up into the sky is a very common one and it means an ascent of the consciousness into a higher world of light and peace.[83]      — SRI AUROBINDO

*

The ladder is of course a symbol of an ascent from one stage to another. The snake indicates an energy, sometimes a good one, more often a bad one (vital or hostile). It may be that the energy was quiescent and therefore not alarming, but by touching it to see how it was you awoke it and you found it was something not safe to handle. There is no clear indication what this energy was. These dream-experiences do not depend on the waking thoughts as do ordinary subconscient dreams which are dreams only and not experiences. They have a life, a structure, an arrangement and forms and meanings of their own; but they are often connected with the

inner condition and experiences or movements of the
sadhana.[84]                                    — Sri Aurobindo

                              *

> *Often I have dreams about railways. I often miss the
> train...*

It is quite symbolical!

> *...because I have too much luggage. I run after it and
> at times I succeed in catching up with it and jumping
> into the last coach.*

The train, the ship, and I suppose the aeroplane also are for
those who do yoga, symbols of the way and of the Force
that leads you — if you lose your time or if you have too
much luggage or if you think of it too late, well, you miss
the way and you must run hard to catch up.[85]

                                              The Mother

                              *

Snakes usually signify bad thoughts or bad will from people
around you — or an adverse attack that can manifest as an
illness. But...if you are not frightened and go on your way
unperturbed, nothing bad will happen to you.[86]

                                              The Mother

                              *

*In dream I saw some people climbing up a mountain with great difficulty. I was also climbing with them. After a time I got tired, so I gave up climbing and began to think what was to be done. Then I felt that a force lifted me up lightly and carried me to the top of the mountain. On reaching the top, I saw that there were many beautiful houses of different colours and lights. Then I woke up. What does this dream signify?*

It is a symbol of the two methods — one of self-effort, the other of the action of the Mother's Force carrying the sadhak.[87]                    — SRI AUROBINDO

# SLEEP, DREAMS AND SADHANA

Sleep cannot be replaced, but it can be changed; for you can become conscious in sleep. If you are thus conscious, then the night can be utilised for a higher working — provided the body gets its due rest; for the object of sleep is the body's rest and the renewal of the vital-physical force.[88]

SRI AUROBINDO

*

Sleep is indispensable in the present state of the body. It is by a progressive control over the subconscient that the sleep can become more and more conscious.[89]     — THE MOTHER

*

If you want to remain conscious at night, train yourself to make your sleep conscious — not to eliminate sleep altogether, but to transform it.[90]     — SRI AUROBINDO

*

*How to make a heavy subconscient sleep light?*

By calling in more consciousness.

*I have noticed that even half an hour's sleep during*

> *day-time refreshes me more than five or six hours' sleep*
> *at night. What is the reason for this?*

It must be because it is a different kind of sleep in the day-time, less heavy, with less time spent in the subconscient.[91]

SRI AUROBINDO

\*

In the waking state you are conscious only of a certain limited field and action of your nature. In sleep you can become vividly aware of things beyond this field — a larger mental or vital nature behind the waking state or else a subtle physical or a subconscient nature which contains much that is there in you but not distinguishably active in the waking state. All these obscure tracts have to be cleared or else there can be no change of Prakriti. You should not allow yourself to be disturbed by the press of vital or subconscient dreams — for these two make up the larger part of dream-experience — but aspire to get rid of these things and of the activities they indicate, to be conscious and reject all but the divine Truth; the more you get that Truth and cling to it in the waking state, rejecting all else, the more all this inferior dream-stuff will get clear.[92]         — SRI AUROBINDO

\*

When you practise yoga, the consciousness opens and you become aware — especially in sleep — of things, scenes, beings, happenings of other (not physical) worlds and your-

self in sleep go there and act there. Very often these things
have an importance for the sadhana. So you need not regret
seeing all this when you sleep or meditate.

But in no case should you fear.[93]          — SRI AUROBINDO

\*

Now the procedure to deal with dreams and the dreamland.
First become conscious — conscious of your dreams. Observe the relation between them and the happenings of your
waking hours. If you remember your night, you will be able
to trace back very often the condition of your day to the
condition of your night. In sleep some action or other is always going on in your mental or vital or other plane; things
happen there and they govern your waking consciousness.
For instance, some are very anxious to perfect themselves
and make a great effort during the day. They go to sleep
and, when they rise the next day, they find no trace of the
gains of their previous day's effort; they have to go over the
same ground once again. This means that the effort and
whatever achievement there was belonged to the more superficial or wakeful parts of the being, but there were deeper
and dormant parts that were not touched. In sleep you fell
into the grip of these unconscious regions and they opened
and swallowed all that you had laboriously built up in your
conscious hours.

Be conscious! Be conscious of the night as well as of the
day. First you have to get consciousness, afterwards, control. You who remember your dreams may have had this
experience that, even while dreaming, you knew it was a

dream; you knew that it was an experience that did not belong to the material world. When once you know, you can act there in the same way as in the material world; even in the dreaming, you can exercise your conscious will and change the whole course of your dream-experience.

And as you become more and more conscious, you will begin to have the same control over your being at night as you have in the day, perhaps even more. For at night you are free, at least partially, from slavery to the mechanism of the body. The control over the processes of the body-consciousness is more difficult, since they are more rigid, less amenable to change than are the mental or the vital processes.[94]

THE MOTHER

*

*Sweet Mother,*

*Is it possible to have control over oneself during sleep? For example, if I want to see you in my dreams, can I do it at will?*

Control during sleep is entirely possible and it is progressive if you persist in the effort. You begin by remembering your dreams, then gradually you remain more and more conscious during your sleep, and not only can you control your dreams but you can guide and organise your activities during sleep.

If you persist in your will and your effort, you are sure to learn how to come and find me at night during your sleep and afterwards to remember what has happened.

For this, two things are necessary, which you must develop by aspiration and by calm and persistent effort.

(1) Concentrate your thought on the will to come and find me; then pursue this thought, first by an effort of imagination, afterwards in a tangible and increasingly real way, until you are in my presence.

(2) Establish a sort of bridge between the waking and the sleeping consciousness, so that when you wake up you remember what has happened.

It may be that you succeed immediately, but more often it takes a certain time and you must persist in the effort.[95]

THE MOTHER

*

*Is it useful to note down one's dreams?*

Yes, for more than a year I applied myself to this kind of self-discipline. I noted down everything — a few words, just a little thing, an impression — and I tried to pass from one memory to another. At first it was not very fruitful, but at the end of about fourteen months I could follow, beginning from the end, all the movements, all the dreams right up to the beginning of the night. That puts you in such a conscious, continuously conscious state that finally I was not sleeping at all. My body lay stretched, deeply asleep, but there was no rest in the consciousness. The result was absolutely wonderful; you become conscious of the different phases of sleep, conscious absolutely of everything that happens there, to the least detail, then nothing can any longer escape your control. But if during the day you have a lot of work and you truly need sleep, I advise you not to try!

In any case, there is one thing altogether indispensable, not to make the least movement when you wake up; you must learn to wake up in a state of complete immobility, otherwise everything disappears.[96]                    — THE MOTHER

*

*During sleep one has often the impression of entering into a region of light, of higher knowledge, but on waking up one brings back only the impression, the memory. Why?*

That is because in the ladder of being which climbs from the most external to the highest consciousness, there are gaps, breaks of continuity, and when the consciousness rises, descends and goes up again, it passes through some kind of dark holes where there is nothing. Then it enters into a sleep, a sort of unconsciousness, and wakes up as best it can on the other side and hardly remembers what it has brought back from above. This is what happens very frequently and particularly in the state called *samādhi*. People who enter into *samādhi* find out that between their active external consciousness and their consciousness in meditation, there lies a blank. Up there, they are almost necessarily conscious — conscious of the state in which they find themselves — but when coming down again towards their body, on the way they enter into a kind of hole where they lose

everything — they are unable to bring back the experience
with them. Quite a discipline is needed to create in oneself
the many steps which enable the consciousness not to forget
what it has experienced up there. It is not an impossible discipline but it is extremely long and requires an unshakable
patience, for it is as if you wanted to build up in you a being,
a body; and for that you require first of all the necessary
knowledge, but also such a prolonged persistence and per-
severance as would discourage many. But it is altogether
indispensable if you want to take part in the knowledge of
your higher being.[97]	— THE MOTHER

\*

*Can one learn to control one's subconscient as one
controls one's conscious thought?*

It is especially during the body's sleep that one is in contact
with the subconscient. In becoming conscious of one's
nights, control of the subconscient becomes much easier.[98]
THE MOTHER

\*

Sleep, because of its subconscient basis, usually brings a
falling down to a lower level, unless it is a conscious sleep;
to make it more and more conscious is the one permanent
remedy: but also until that is done, one should always react
against this sinking tendency when one wakes and not allow
the effect of dull nights to accumulate. But these things need

always a settled endeavour and discipline and must take time, sometimes a long time. It will not do to refrain from the effort because immediate results do not appear.[99]

SRI AUROBINDO

\*

The consciousness in the night almost always descends below the level of what one has gained by sadhana in the waking consciousness, unless there are special experiences of an uplifting character in the time of sleep or unless the yogic consciousness acquired is so strong in the physical itself as to counteract the pull of the subconscient inertia. In ordinary sleep the consciousness in the body is that of the subconscient physical, which is a diminished consciousness, not awake and alive like the rest of the being. The rest of the being stands back and part of its consciousness goes out into other planes and regions and has experiences which are recorded in dreams such as that you have related. You say you go to very bad places and have experiences like the one you narrate; but that is not a sign, necessarily, of anything wrong in you. It merely means that you go into the vital world, as everybody does, and the vital world is full of such places and such experiences. What you have to do is not so much to avoid at all going there, for it cannot be avoided altogether, but to go with full protection until you get mastery in these regions of supraphysical Nature.[100]

SRI AUROBINDO

\*

The difficulty of keeping the consciousness at night happens to most — it is because the night is the time of sleep and relaxation and the subconscient comes up. The true consciousness comes at first in the waking state or in meditation, it takes possession of the mental, the vital, the conscious physical, but the subconscious vital and physical remain obscure and this obscurity comes up when there is sleep or an inert relaxation. When the subconscient is enlightened and penetrated by the true consciousness this disparity disappears.[101]
                                                        — SRI AUROBINDO

*

At night when one sinks into the subconscient after being in a good state of consciousness we find that state gone and we have to labour to get it back again. On the other hand, if the sleep is of the better kind one may wake up in a good condition. Of course, it is better to be conscious in sleep, if one can.[102]
                                                        — SRI AUROBINDO

*

… it is a well-known psychological law that what is suppressed or rejected in the waking state may still recur in sleep and dream because they are still there in the subconscient being. But if the waking state is thoroughly cleared, these dream-movements must gradually disappear because they lose their food and the impressions in the subconscient are gradually effaced. This is the cause of the dreams of which you are so much afraid. You should see

that they are only a subordinate symptom which need not
alarm you if you can once get control of your waking condition.[103]                                          — SRI AUROBINDO

\*

The sleep consciousness can be effectively dealt with only
when the waking mind has made a certain amount of
progress.[104]                                      — SRI AUROBINDO

\*

It is usually only if there is much activity of sadhana in the
day that it extends also into the sleep-state.[105]

SRI AUROBINDO

\*

About unconsciousness coming in in sleep: This is quite
usual. Consciousness in sleep can only be gradually established with the growth of the true consciousness in the waking state.[106]                                     — SRI AUROBINDO

\*

*If one is more conscious in the day, one will have dreams
of a good kind?*

It is very difficult to say on what it depends.

It happens that when you need to dream of something, so

that it may enlighten you on a point of your nature, give you an indication about the effort you must make, it comes.

It depends perhaps on a consciousness that watches over everyone; and provided one is just a little open, it can guide him and give sure indications.

I think there is an entire category of dreams which are absolutely commonplace, useless and simply tiring, which one can avoid if, before going to sleep, one makes a little effort of concentration, tries to put himself in contact with what is best in him, by either an aspiration or a prayer, and to sleep only after this is done… even, if one likes, try to meditate and pass quite naturally from meditation into sleep without even realising it… Usually there is a whole category of dreams which are useless, tiring, which prevent you from resting well — all this might be avoided. And then, if one has truly succeeded well in his concentration, it is quite possible that one may have, at night, not exactly dreams but experiences of which one becomes conscious and which are very useful, indications, as I just told you, indications about questions you asked yourself and of which you did not have the answers; or else a set of circumstances where you ought to take a decision and don't know what decision to take; or else some way of being of your own character which does not show itself to you clearly in the waking consciousness — because you are so accustomed to it that you are not aware of it — but something that harms your development and obscures your consciousness, and which appears to you in a symbolic revelatory dream, and you become clearly aware of the thing, then you can act upon it. It depends not on what one was during the day, because this doesn't always have much effect upon the night, but on the way one has gone to sleep. It is enough just to have at the moment of sleeping a sincere aspiration that the night, instead of being a darkening of the consciousness, may be a help to understand something, to have an experience; and then, though it doesn't come always, it has a chance of coming.

There is also, you know, a whole lot of activities of the night which one doesn't remember at all. Sometimes when one has awakened quite slowly and quietly, when one hasn't jumped up while awakening, when one wakes up quite gently, quite slowly, without stirring, one has a vague impression of something that has happened which has left an imprint on one's consciousness — you have your own way of waking up — particular, sometimes even strange. And so if you remain very quiet and observe attentively, without moving, you notice a kind of half-memory of an activity that took place at night, and if you remain concentrated on it, still motionless for some time, suddenly it may come back like that, like something that appears from behind a veil, and you can get hold of the tail of a dream. When you hold the tail — just a little event — when you hold the tail, you pull it, like this, very gently, and it comes. But you must be very quiet and must not move. And usually these dreams are very interesting; these activities are very instructive.

One does lots and lots of things at night which one doesn't know, and if one learns, you see, when one becomes conscious, one can begin to have control. Before being conscious you have no control at all. But when you begin to be conscious, you can also begin to have a control. And then if you have control of your activities of the night, you can sleep much better; for the fact that when you wake up you are often at least as tired as when going to bed and have a feeling of lassitude shows that you do any number of useless things during the night; you tire yourself running around in the vital worlds or moving in the mind in a frantic activity. So when you get up you feel tired.

Well, once you have the control you can stop that completely... stop it before going to sleep... make yourself like a vast sea, that is, it is completely calm and still and vast... well, you can make your mind like that, vast, calm, like a flat, motionless surface; then your sleep is excellent.

Of course, here too it is a question of people going in their sleep to places of the vital worlds which are very bad, and then, when they return, sometimes they are more than tired, at times they are ill, or they are absolutely exhausted. This is because they were in bad places and had a fight. But this surely has something to do with the state of the consciousness during the waking hours. If, for example, you have been angry during the day, you see, there are many chances that at night you will be in a vital fight for some time. This happens.[107]

— THE MOTHER

*

To sleep well the vital and physical and mind also must learn how to relax themselves and be quiet.[108]  — SRI AUROBINDO

*

*I would like to know why I had such a disturbed night.*

Obviously you did not quiet your thoughts before going to sleep. At the time of lying down one should always begin by quieting one's thoughts.[109]          — THE MOTHER

*

There is no end to the discoveries that you can make in dreams. But one thing is very important: never go to sleep when you are very tired, for if you do, you fall into a sort of unconsciousness and dreams do with you whatever they like, without your being able to exercise the least control. Just as you should always rest before eating, I would advise you all to rest before going to sleep. But then you must know how to rest.

There are many ways of doing it. Here is one: first of all, put your body at ease, comfortably stretched out on a bed or in an easy-chair. Then try to relax your nerves, all together or one by one, till you have obtained complete relaxation. This done, and while your body lies limp like a rag on the bed, make your brain silent and immobile, till it is no longer conscious of itself. Then slowly, imperceptibly, pass from this state into sleep. When you wake up the next morning, you will be full of energy. On the contrary, if you go to bed completely tired and without relaxing yourself, you will fall into a heavy, dull and unconscious sleep in which the vital will lose all its energies.

It is possible that you may not obtain an immediate result, but persevere.[110]          — THE MOTHER

*

At night, you have to pass into sleep in the concentration —
you must be able to concentrate with the eyes closed, lying
down and the concentration must deepen into sleep — that
is to say, sleep must become a concentrated going inside
away from the outer waking state. If you find it necessary to
sit for a time you may do so, but afterwards lie down keeping the concentration till this happens.[111] — SRI AUROBINDO

*

*I have noticed one thing: When I sit for a few minutes
and make an effort to concentrate before going to sleep,
the next day I wake up quite early and am quite fresh. I
concentrate on the tiny luminous tip of an incense-stick.
But how is it that I wake up early because of that? There
is no relation between these two things!*

On the contrary, there is a very concrete relation. When you
concentrate before sleeping, then in your sleep you remain
in contact with the Divine force; but when you fall heavily
to sleep without any preliminary concentration, you sink
into the inconscient and the sleep is more tiring than restful,
and it is difficult to come out of this sluggishness.[112]

THE MOTHER

*

*At times I talk in my sleep. It is a sign that the mind
lacks control, isn't it? So what should I do to keep it
quiet at night?*

Generally when the body is asleep at night, the mind goes out because it is difficult for it to remain quiet for a long time; and that is why most people do not talk.

But your mind seems to remain in your body, so you must ask it to remain perfectly quiet and silent so that your body can rest properly. A little concentration for that, before going to sleep, will surely be effective.[113]                    — THE MOTHER

\*

[To be conscious in sleep:] You have to start by concentrating before you sleep always with a specific will or aspiration. The will or aspiration may take time to reach the subconscient, but if it is sincere, strong and steady, it does reach after a time — so that an automatic consciousness and will are established in the sleep itself which will do what is necessary.[114]                          — SRI AUROBINDO

\*

> *Sweet Mother, to profit by one's nights, to have good dreams, is it necessary that one should have done nothing very intellectual late at night, or that one should not eat too late at night or do anything external?*

This depends on each one; but certainly if you want to sleep quietly at night, you must not study till just before sleeping. If you read something which requires concentration, your head will continue to work and so you won't sleep well. When the mind continues working one doesn't rest.

The ideal, you see, is to enter an integral repose, that is, immobility in the body, perfect peace in the vital, absolute silence in the mind — and the consciousness goes out of all activity to enter into Sachchidananda. If you can do this, then when you wake up you get up with the feeling of an extraordinary power, a perfect joy. But it is not very, very easy to do this. It can be done; this is the ideal condition.

Usually it is not at all like this, and most of the time almost all the hours of sleep are wasted in some kind of disordered activities; your body begins to toss about in your bed, you give kicks, you turn, you start, you turn this way and that, and then you do this (*gesture*) and then this... So you don't rest at all.[115]                    — THE MOTHER

\*

*What is the way to take rest before going to sleep?*

There are many methods, but I will give you one. First, your body must be comfortable, on a bed, in an easy-chair — anywhere so long as it is comfortable. Then you learn how to relax your nerves one after the other, unntil you achieve complete relaxation. You should relax all your nerves — you can relax them all together, but perhaps it is easier to relax them one after the other, and this becomes very interesting. And when that is done, you must make your brain quiet and silent and at the same time keep your body like a rag on the bed. You must make the brain so still and absolutely quiet that it is not aware of itself. And then, don't *try* to sleep, but pass very gently from this state into sleep without being aware of it. When you wake up the next morning you will be full of energy. But if you go to bed very tired and without even trying to relax, to calm down, you will fall into a heavy, dull and unconscious sleep and the vital will lose all its energy. Perhaps this won't have any immediate effect, but it is better to try it than to plunge into sleep when you are very tired.

If you relax very gently before going to sleep, you will feel great pleasure in going to sleep. If you manage to relax the nerves, even of only one arm or leg, you will see how pleasant it is. If you go to sleep with your nerves tense, you will have a very restless sleep and change position very often during the night. That kind of rest is no good.[116]

THE MOTHER

\*

*Why does one wake up tired in the morning, and what should one do to have a better sleep?*

If you wake up tired in the morning, it is because of *tamas*, nothing else, a formidable mass of *tamas*. I myself noticed it when I began to do the yoga of the body. It is inevitable so long as the body is not transformed.

[When going to sleep] You must lie flat on your back and relax all the muscles and all the nerves — it is an easy thing to learn — to be like what I call a rag on a bed: nothing else remains. And if you can do that with the mind also, you get rid of all those stupid dreams that make you more tired when you get up than when you went to bed. It is the cellular activity of the brain that continues without control, and that tires one much. So, a total relaxation, a sort of complete calm, without tension, in which everything is stopped. But this is only the beginning.

Afterwards, you make a self-giving as total as possible, of everything, from top to bottom, from outside to inside, and an eradication, as total as possible, of all the resistance of the ego. And you begin repeating your mantra — your mantra, if you have one, or any word which has a power for you, a word leaping forth from the heart spontaneously, like a prayer, a word which sums up your aspiration. After repeating it a certain number of times, if you are accustomed to do so, you enter into trance. And from that trance you pass into sleep. The trance lasts as long as it should and quite naturally, spontaneously, you pass into sleep. But when you come back from this sleep, you remember everything; the sleep was like a continuation of the trance.

Fundamentally, the sole purpose of sleep is to enable the body to assimilate the effect of the trance so that the effect may be received everywhere, and to enable the body to do its natural nocturnal function of eliminating toxins. And when you wake up, there is not that trace of heaviness which comes from sleep: the effect of the trance continues.

Even for those who have never been in trance, it is good to repeat a mantra, a word, a prayer before going into sleep. But there must be a life in the words; I do not mean an intellectual significance, nothing of that kind, but a vibration. And its effect on the body is extraordinary: it begins to vibrate, vibrate, vibrate... and quietly you let yourself go, as though you wanted to go to sleep. The body vibrates more and more,

more and more, more and more, and away you go. That is the cure for tamas.

It is tamas which causes bad sleep. There are two kinds of bad sleep: the sleep that makes you heavy, dull, as if you lost all the effect of the effort you put in during the preceding day; and the sleep that exhausts you as if you had passed your time in fighting. I have noticed that if you cut your sleep into slices (it is a habit one can form), the nights become better. That is to say, you must be able to come back to your normal consciousness and normal aspiration at fixed inter- vals — come back at the call of the consciousness. But for that you must not use an alarm-clock! When you are in trance, it is not good to be shaken out of it.

When you are about to go to sleep, you can make a forma- tion; say: "I shall wake up at such an hour" (you do that very well when you are a child). For the first stretch of sleep you must count at least three hours; for the last, one hour is suffi- cient. But the first one must be three hours at the minimum. On the whole, you have to remain in bed at least seven hours; in six hours you do not have time enough to do much (natu- rally I am looking at it from the point of view of sadhana) to make the nights useful.

To make use of the nights is an excellent thing. It has a double effect: a negative effect, it prevents you from falling backward, losing what you have gained — that is indeed pain- ful — and a positive effect, you make some progress, you continue your progress. You make use of the night, so there is no trace of fatigue any more.

Two things you must eliminate: falling into the stupor of the inconscience, with all the things of the subconscient and

inconscient that rise up, invade you, enter you; and a vital
and mental superactivity where you pass your time in fighting, literally, terrible battles. People come out of that state
bruised, as if they had received blows. And they did receive
them — it is not "as if"! And I see only one way out: to
change the nature of sleep.[117]                    — THE MOTHER

*

*Mother, what does this mean: "sleep has to be gradually
transformed into the yogic repose"?*

Ah, yogic repose. It means that instead of an unconscious
sleep it is a sleep — if you want to call it sleep — a conscious sleep. The body is in a state of complete repose, with
the nerves relaxed, the muscles relaxed; one is completely
relaxed and at rest; but the spirit remains conscious, conscious enough to be able to put the vital also at rest, the
mind also at rest, and let everything be in a state of peace,
quietude, immobility, so that the consciousness may be completely free. Then the consciousness can either rest also, if it
thinks it necessary, or work if it thinks that is needed; and in
any case it is free to do as it wants, what it wants, and to go
to the regions to which it wants to go. But the parts belonging to the present physical being, that is, the mind, vital and
physical, are in a complete repose and a kind of immobility,
due to which the hours of sleep do not need to be so long.
One can cut short the number of hours of sleep very much
if one leaves the body in this state of rest. But this asks
for much work, and a very conscious work, you see, very

conscious and very persistent. It cannot be had immediately, it may require years of discipline. Only, once it is acquired, well, one has mastered sleep and can prevent, well... For example, there are many people who, when they go to sleep, are in a very good state of consciousness, and when they wake up in the morning they are completely dazed and have lost all that they had gained the previous day; and that's because their sleep is unconscious and they go out in the vital or the mind or the subtle physical; they go to undesirable places or else fall into the inconscience and lose in this inconscience all they had gained before... It is something very necessary, but it can't be acquired very easily. It is one of the most difficult things to do, but it is very useful; only, one can hardly do it without a very close guidance, because unless one knows how to do it even to the last detail, one risks doing stupid things.

In any case one thing you can do in all security is, before going to sleep, to concentrate, relax all tension in the physical being, try... that is, in the body try so that the body lies like a soft rag on the bed, that it is no longer something with twitchings and cramps; to relax it completely as though it were a kind of thing like a rag. And then, the vital: to calm it, calm it as much as you can, make it as quiet, as peaceful as possible. And then the mind also — the mind, try to keep it like that, without any activity. You must put upon the brain the force of great peace, great quietude, of silence if possible, and not follow ideas actively, not make any effort, nothing, nothing; you must relax all movement there too, but relax it in a kind of silence and quietude as great as possible.

Once you have done all this, you may add either a prayer

or an aspiration in accordance with your nature, to ask for the consciousness and peace and to be protected against all the adverse forces throughout the sleep, to be in a concentration of quiet aspiration and in the protection; ask the Grace to watch over your sleep; and then go to sleep. This is to sleep in the best possible conditions. What happens afterwards depends on your inner impulses, but if you do this persistently, night after night, night after night, after some time it will have its effect.

Usually, you see, one lies down on the bed and tries to sleep as quickly as possible, and then, that's all, with a state of total ignorance of how it ought to be done. But what I have just told you, if you do that regularly it will have an effect. In any case, it can very well avoid the attacks which occur at night: one has gone to bed very nicely, one wakes up ill; this is something absolutely disastrous, it means that during the night one has been getting infected somewhere in a state of total inconscience.[118]     — THE MOTHER

\*

*May I try to make my nights conscious? I pray for guidance.*

1) A short concentration before going to sleep, with an aspiration to remember the activities of the night when you wake up.

2) When you wake up, do not make any sudden movement of the head and keep still for a few minutes, with a concentration to remember what happened during your sleep.

3) Repeat these exercises every day until you begin to perceive a result.[119] — THE MOTHER

\*

All dream or sleep consciousness cannot be converted at once into conscious sadhana. That has to be done progressively.[120] — SRI AUROBINDO

\*

# APPENDIX I

## On Dreams*

At first sight one might think that the subject of dreams is an altogether secondary one; this activity generally seems to have very little importance compared to the activity of our waking state.

However, if we examine the question a little more closely, we shall see that this is not at all the case.

To begin with, we should remember that more than one third of our existence is spent in sleeping and that, consequently, the time devoted to physical sleep well deserves our attention.

I say physical sleep, for it would be wrong to think that our whole being sleeps when our bodies are asleep.

A study based on certain experiments conducted according to the strictest scientific methods, was published some twenty years ago by Dr. Vaschid in a book entitled "Sleep and Dreams".

The doctors who carried out these experiments were led to the conclusion that mental activity never really ceases; and it is this activity which is more or less confusedly transcribed in our brains by what we know as dreams. Thus, whether we are aware of it or not, we always dream.

Certainly, it is possible to suppress this activity completely and to have a total, dreamless sleep; but to be able in this

* The Mother, *Words of Long Ago*, Collected Works of the Mother, Centenary Edition, Vol. 2, pp. 30-37.

way to immerse our mental being in a repose similar to the repose of our physical being, we must have achieved a perfect control over it, and this is not an easy thing to do.

In most cases, this activity is even heightened, because, as the body is asleep, the internal faculties are no longer focussed on or used by the physical life.

It is sometimes said that in a man's sleep his true nature is revealed.

Indeed, it often happens that the sensory being, which throughout the whole day has been subjected to the control of the active will, reacts all the more violently during the night when this constraint is no longer effective.

All the desires that have been repressed without being dissolved — and this dissociation can only be obtained after much sound and wide-ranging analysis — seek satisfaction while the will is dormant.

And since desires are true dynamic centres of formation, they tend to organise, within and around us, the combination of circumstances that is most favourable to their satisfaction.

In this way the fruit of many efforts made by our conscious thought during the day can be destroyed in a few hours at night.

This is one of the main causes of the resistances which our will for progress often encounters within us, of the difficulties which sometimes appear insurmountable to us and which we are unable to explain, because our goodwill seems so integral to us.

We must therefore learn to know our dreams, and first of all to distinguish between them, for they are very varied in nature and quality. In the course of one night we may often have several dreams which belong to different categories, depending on the depth of our sleep.

As a general rule, each individual has a period of the night that is more favourable for dreams, during which his activity is more fertile, more intellectual, and the mental circumstances of the environment in which he moves are more interesting.

The great majority of dreams have no other value than that of a purely mechanical and uncontrolled activity of the physical brain, in which certain cells continue to function during sleep as generators of sensory images and impressions conforming to the pictures received from outside.

These dreams are nearly always caused by purely physical circumstances — state of health, digestion, position in bed, etc.

With a little self-observation and a few precautions, it is easy to avoid this type of dream, which is as useless as it is tiring, by eliminating its physical causes.

There are also other dreams which are nothing but futile manifestations of the erratic activities of certain mental faculties, which associate ideas, conversations and memories that come together at random.

Such dreams are already more significant, for these erratic activities reveal to us the confusion that prevails in our mental being as soon as it is no longer subject to the control of our will, and show us that this being is still not organised or ordered within us, that it is not mature enough to have an autonomous life.

Almost the same in form to these, but more important in

their consequences, are the dreams which I mentioned just now, those which arise from the inner being seeking revenge when it is freed for a moment from the constraint that we impose upon it. These dreams often enable us to perceive tendencies, inclinations, impulses, desires of which we were not conscious so long as our will to realise our ideal kept them concealed in some obscure recess of our being.

You will easily understand that rather than letting them live on unknown to us, it is better to bring them boldly and courageously to the light, so as to force them to leave us for ever.

We should therefore observe our dreams attentively; they are often useful instructors who can give us a powerful help on our way towards self-conquest.

No one knows himself well who does not know the unconfined activities of his nights, and no man can call himself his own master unless he has the perfect consciousness and mastery of the numerous actions he performs during his physical sleep.

But dreams are not merely the malignant informers of our weaknesses or the malicious destroyers of our daily effort for progress.

Although there are dreams which we should contend with or transform, there are others which should on the contrary be cultivated as precious auxiliaries in our work within and around us.

There can be no doubt that from many points of view our subconscient knows more than our habitual consciousness.

Who has not had the experience of a metaphysical, moral or practical problem with which we grapple in vain in the evening, and whose solution, impossible to find then, appears clearly and accurately in the morning on waking?

The mental enquiry had been going on throughout the period of sleep and the internal faculties, freed from all material activity, were able to concentrate solely on the subject of their interest.

Very often, the work itself remains unconscious; only the result is perceived.

But at other times, by means of a dream, we participate in all the mental activity in its smallest details. Only the cerebral transcription of this activity is often so childish that we normally pay no attention to it.

From this point of view, it is interesting to note that there is nearly always a considerable disparity between what our mental activity is in fact and the way in which we perceive it, and especially the way in which we remain conscious of it. In its own medium, this activity produces vibrations which are transmitted by repercussion to the cellular system of our organic brain, but in our sleeping brain, the subtle vibrations of the suprasensible domain can affect only a very limited number of cells; the inertia of most of the organic supports of the cerebral phenomenon reduces the number of active elements, impoverishes the mental synthesis and makes it unfit to transcribe the activity of the internal states, except into images which are most often vague and inadequate.

To make this disparity more tangible to you, I shall give you an example, one among many, which has come to my knowledge.

Recently, a writer was preoccupied with a half-written chapter which he was unable to finish.

His mind, particularly interested in this work of composition, continued the chapter during the night, and the more it phrased and rephrased the ideas making up the various graphs, it became aware that these ideas were not expressed in the most rational order and that the paragraphs had to be rearranged.

All this work was transcribed in the consciousness of our writer in the following dream: he was in his study with several armchairs which he had just brought there and was arranging and rearranging them in the room, until he found the most suitable place for each one.

In the knowledge that certain people may have had of such inadequate transcriptions, we can find the origin of the popular beliefs, the "dream-books" which are the delight of so many simple souls.

But it is easy to understand that this clumsy transcription has a particular form for each individual; each one makes his own distortion.

Consequently, an excessive generalisation of certain interpretations which may have been quite correct for the person applying them to his own case, merely gives rise to vulgar and foolish superstitions.

It is as if the writer we have just mentioned were to impart as a great secret to his friends and acquaintances that every time they saw themselves arranging armchairs in a dream, it was a sign that the next day they would at some moment reverse the order of the paragraphs in a book.

The cerebral transcription of the activities of the night is sometimes warped to such an extent that phenomena are perceived as the opposite of what they really are.

For example, when you have a bad thought against some-one and when this bad thought, left to itself, gathers full force during the night, you dream that the person in question is beating you, is doing you some bad turn, or even wounding you or trying to kill you.

Moreover, as a general rule, we should take great intel-lectual precautions before interpreting a dream, and above all, we should review exhaustively all the subjective ex-planations before we assign to it the value of an objective reality.

However, especially in those who have unlearnt the habit of always directing their thoughts towards themselves, there are cases where we can observe events outside ourselves, events which are not the reflection of our personal mental constructions. And if we know how to translate into intellec-tual language the more or less inadequate images into which the brain has translated these events, we can learn many things that our too limited physical faculties do not allow us to per-ceive.

Some people, by a special culture and training, are even able to become and remain conscious of the deeper activities of their inner being, independently of their own cerebral tran-scription, and thus to evoke them and know them in the wak-ing state with the full range of their faculties.

Many interesting observations could be made on this topic, but perhaps it is better to allow each one to experience for himself the many possibilities which lie within man's reach in a field of activity which he too often leaves undeve-loped.

Uncultivated lands produce weeds. We do not want any

weeds in ourselves, so let us cultivate the vast field of our nights.

You must not think that this can be in the least harmful to the depth of your sleep and the efficacy of a repose which is not only indispensable but beneficial. On the contrary, there are many people whose nights are more tiring than their days, for reasons which often elude them; they should become conscious of these reasons so that their will can begin to act on them and remove their effects, that is, to put a stop to these activities which in such cases are nearly always useless and even harmful.

If our night has enabled us to gain some new knowledge — the solution of a problem, a contact of our inner being with some centre of life or light, or even the accomplishment of some useful task — we shall always wake up with a feeling of strength and well-being.

The hours that are wasted in doing nothing good or useful are the most tiring.

But how can we cultivate this field of action, how can we become conscious of our nocturnal activities?

We shall find the way to do so very broadly outlined in a passage from a book devoted to the study of our inner life:

"The same discipline of concentration which enables man not to remain a stranger to the inner activities of the waking state also provides him with a way to escape from his ignorance of the even richer activities of the various states of sleep.

"These activities usually leave behind them only a few rare and confused memories.

"However, it is noteworthy that a chance circumstance, an impression received, a word pronounced, is sometimes

enough to bring suddenly back to the consciousness a whole
long dream of which we had no recollection a moment before.

"We can infer from this simple fact that the conscious activity has taken only a very minor part in the phenomena of the
sleeping state, since in the normal state of things they would
have remained lost for ever in the subconscient memory.

"In this domain, the practice of concentration should therefore focus both on the special faculty of memory and on the
participation of the consciousness in the activities of the sleeping state.

"Someone who wishes to recover the memory of a forgotten dream should first of all focus his attention on the vague
impressions which the dream may have left behind it and in
this way follow its indistinct trace as far as possible.

"This regular exercise will enable him to go further every
day towards the obscure retreat of the subconscient where
these forgotten phenomena of sleep take refuge, and thus trace
out an easily followed path between these two domains of
consciousness.

"One useful remark to be made from this point of view is
that the absence of memories is very often due to the abrupt-
ness of the return to the waking consciousness. (The waking
should not be too abrupt.)

"As a matter of fact, at that moment, the new activities
breaking into the field of consciousness force out everything
that is unfamiliar to them and add to the difficulty of the
subsequent work of concentration needed to recall the things
which have been expelled in this way. On the other hand,
this work will be made easier whenever certain mental and

even physical precautions are observed for a quiet transition from one state to another. (If possible, do not make any abrupt movements in bed at the time of waking.)

"However, this special training of the faculty of memory can only transform into conscious phenomena in the waking state the phenomena which have already been made conscious, even if only fleetingly, during sleep. For where there is no consciousness, there can be no memory.

"Consequently, in the second place, we must work to extend the participation of the consciousness to a greater number of activities in the sleeping state.

"The daily habit of reviewing with interest the various dreams of the night, whose traces will gradually become transformed into precise memories, as well as the habit of noting them down on waking, will be found most helpful from this point of view.

"By these habits, the mental faculties will be led to adapt their mechanism to phenomena of this kind and to exercise on them their attention, their curiosity and power of analysis.

"A kind of intellectualisation of our dreams will then occur, with the double result of making the conscious activities intervene more and more closely in the play of the formerly disorganised activities of the sleeping state, and of progressively increasing their scope by making them more and more rational and instructive.

"Dreams will then take on the nature of precise visions and sometimes of revelations, and useful knowledge of a whole important order of things will be gained."

25 March 1912

# APPENDIX II

## Three Dreams*

### 1

We were on the summit of a mountain, so high that the valleys were invisible. The sky was perfectly clear and colourless. The summit of the mountain was covered with rich pastures. In these pastures, four herds of cows were grazing, guarded by four cowherds. These herds were at an equal distance from one another, thus forming approximately the four corners of a square. Each guardian had his own very particular appearance and characteristics. "He" was seeking something that he wanted to express and make effective, and for this he lacked certain elements. These elements lay beyond the summit of the mountain and He was asking me if there was any way of going there to fetch them. The question was voiced aloud and all the cows of the herd that was nearest to us bounded towards Him, lowing with delight. The man who was leading them, tall, strong, stocky, clothed in animal skins, white-skinned and very hairy, with black, shaggy hair and a square face, went towards Him and said to Him in a loud voice, "I put myself entirely at your disposal, my cows want to serve you and so do I. I shall lead them to the place where the elements of knowledge you want to acquire are lying and we shall bring them to you."

* The Mother, *Words of Long Ago*, Collected Works of the Mother, Centenary Edition, Vol. 2, pp. 131-36.

While he was speaking, the herd which was on the right in the same line drew near, led by its guardian, who was interested and came to listen. He was tall, thin, sumptuously dressed, with smooth skin, an oval, elongated face and very black and silky hair falling to his shoulders. One part of his garment was red, but there were several other colours. He was friendly and well disposed. But he did not offer his services.

*2 August 1914*

## 2

We were advancing along the broad white highway which led to our goal, when at a fork in the road we saw a great number of people massing and huddling together with expressions of terror. We wonder why as we proceed on our way, when we hear ourselves being called by a shepherd dressed in white, who tells us to join the people on the bank by the roadside. And in answer to our enquiry, he tells us that an enormous herd of cows and bulls has been kept prisoner until now, but that the time has come to let them loose, that the rope which is holding them back will be removed, and that they are going to charge and are likely to destroy everything in their path. I reply, "Indeed these creatures are full of vigour and sometimes even of apparently blind violence, but for people such as we two who are walking straight on our way, there is nothing to fear; bulls have never done us any harm." But the shepherd insists, saying that it is really something exceptional and unprecedented. So as not to vex him we stop and stand by the roadside in front of the crowding people. But there again he insists, saying, "Not there, not there, you will be trampled down, behind." And he makes us stand behind all the others, back from the side of the road.

At that moment, in the distance, I catch sight of the immense herd of cows and bulls; the rope that held them back is removed and they surge forward, charging straight in front of them; and if anyone had been in their path, they would certainly have trampled him down. When all have passed, the leader of the herd, who had been kept until last, is let loose. He is a splendid, enormous white bull. Instead of following the same path as the others, he turns to the right, in front of us, following the descending path. But after a moment he stops, looking for something, does not find it, retraces his steps, and finally stations himself just in front of me. Then I see that it is a triple bull, composed of three bulls closely bound together. One of the three (the middle one, I think) was a little less white than the two others. To my left there was a priest who, at the sight of this enormous creature charging upon us and halting just in front of me, is seized with a great fear. And in his fright he begins to move restlessly. Then I say to him, "Well then, what about your faith in God? If He has decided that you are to be trampled down by this bull, won't you find that His will is good?" Rather ashamed of himself, he wants to look brave, so he starts talking to the bull and giving him friendly pats on the muzzle. But the powerful creature was beginning to lose patience. And I was thinking, "With his fear, this fool will really end up by causing a disaster." "We had better go away," I said, turning towards "Him". And without any further care for the bull, we set out on our way once more. We have scarcely taken a few steps on the road when we see the bull quietly passing beside us, calm and strong. A little farther on, I see another bull coming in the opposite direction, all reddish-brown, with a wild and ferocious look, charging with its huge horns pointed forward. I look back towards "Him", walking a few steps behind me, and I say to him, "This one is the really dangerous creature, the one that is alone and going in the opposite direction to the others. This one has evil intentions. It cannot even see us because we are on the straight path and are protected. But I am much afraid for the others." Still a little farther on we hear a galloping sound behind us, as if the ferocious bull were coming back with others. I feel that it is time for us to reach the goal. At that moment the road seems to be closed; in front of us there is a door that I want to open, but my hand slips on the knob and I cannot turn it. And yet time is pressing. Then I distinctly hear the deep Voice, "Look." I look up, and right in front of us, beside the closed door, I see a wide-open door leading into a square room which is the goal. And the voice resumes, "Enter. That is where all the doors are to be found and you will be able to open them all."

With a feeling of great peace and tranquil strength I woke up.

*1914 (after August)*

### 3

Lord, last night you gave me a dream.

This is what I remember of it:

At the top of a very high tower standing on a high mountain, in a room so vast that it seemed to be low, I was leaning against the far wall, and facing me was a window looking outside. On my left a raised throne with several steps, and on the throne sat the Lord of Nations.[1] This I knew although I had not looked at him. To my right at the far end of the immense room, in a kind of alcove lit from above, sat a young woman — a nation. She was a small, dumpy child with very dark hair and a pale and mat complexion. She had put on a wedding-dress, with a crown of white flowers on her head (the dress was mostly white with some blue and a few touches of gold). I knew that I had helped this nation to dress in this way, and to climb the mountain and the tower to come up to the room. She had come to offer herself as a bride to the Lord of Nations, and for this purpose she was to undergo a series of ordeals that the Lord wanted to impose upon her in order to know whether she was worthy of him. These ordeals were the ordeals of Terror.

For the first ordeal he had a full glass as well as a decanter brought to her. And she was to drink the contents of both. To her they seemed to be blood — human blood newly shed. And He, from the height of his throne, was saying to her, "Drink this blood to show that you are not afraid." The

---

[1] The Lord of Nations is an asura, that is, a hostile being of the mentalised vital plane. Of him the Mother said in 1953: "Even now, among the beings who are concerned with the earth, the asuric beings, the greatest of the asuras who is still busy with the earth at present, who is the asura of falsehood and calls himself the 'Lord of Nations' — he has taken a beautiful name, he is Lord of Nations — it is he, wherever there is something going wrong, you may be sure it is he or a representive of his who is there."

*Questions and Answers 1953* (10 June), p. 98.

poor child was trembling with disgust and did not dare touch the ghastly beverage. But at that hour, Lord, You had given me the full consciousness and power of the Truth. From where I stood I could clearly see the transparent purity of the water which the glass and the decanter really contained. And while the child was still hesitating and the Lord was taunting her in a biting tone, "What! you are trembling already! This is yet only the first ordeal, the easiest of all, what will you do next?"

Then, heedless of the consequences, I cried to the child *in a language that the Lord did not understand*, "You can drink without fear, it is only water, pure water, I swear it." And the child, trusting in my word that dispelled the suggestion, began to drink calmly....

But because of the force with which I had spoken, the Lord suspected something and turned towards me in fury, rebuking me for speaking when I should not. To which I replied — still heedless of the consequences which I knew to be inevitable — "What I say is not your concern since You cannot understand the language I have used!"....

Then the memorable thing happened....

The room suddenly grew as dark as night and in this night a still darker form appeared, a form I perceived distinctly although no one else could see it.

This form of darkness was like the shadow of the light of Truth within me. And this shadow was Terror.

Immediately the fight began. The being, whose hair was like furious serpents, moving with hideous contortions and terrible gnashing of teeth, rushed upon me. If with only one of her fingers she were to touch my breast at the place of the heart *the great calamity for the world* would occur, and this had to be avoided at all costs. It was a fearful battle. All the powers of Truth were concentrated in my consciousness; and nothing less was needed to fight against so formidable a foe as Terror!

Her endurance and strength in combat were remarkable. At last came the supreme moment of the fight. We were so close to each other that it seemed impossible that we should not touch, and her outstretched finger drew nearer, threatening my breast....

At that precise moment the Lord of Nations, who could see nothing of the tragic battle, stretched out his hand to take something from a small table at his side. This hand — unawares — passed between my opponent and myself. I was then able to take support from it and Terror, for this time definitely vanquished, sank to the ground like a dark dust without power or reality....

Then, recognising the one who sat on the throne, and doing homage to his power, I leant my head upon his shoulder and said to him joyfully, "Together, we have conquered Terror!"

Such was my dream — and with it You gave me the full understanding of it.

For all this I give thanks to You, as for a priceless gift.

*31 January-1 February [1915?]*

# GLOSSARY

*The Glossary includes Sanskrit terms and special terms found in Sri Aurobindo's writings. Explanations of philosophical and psychological terms have generally been given in Sri Aurobindo's own words.*

**Ananda** — bliss, delight, beatitude, spiritual ecstacy; the essential principle of delight: a self-delight which is the very nature of the transcendent and infinite existence.

**Brahmaloka** — world of the *brahman*, the Supreme Being, in which the soul is one with the infinite existence.

**Consciousness** — the self-aware force of existence. The essence of consciousness is the power to be aware of itself and its objects; but it is not only power of awareness of self and things, it is or has also a dynamic and creative energy. Consciousness is not synonymous with mentality, which is only a middle term; below mentality, it sinks into vital and material movements which are for us subconscient; above, it rises into the Supramental which is for us the superconscient.

**Divine, the** — the Supreme Truth, the Supreme Being from whom all have come and in whom all are.
**Divine Force** — *see* **Force, the**

**Force, the** — the Divine Force, the one Energy that alone exists and alone makes universal or individual action possible, for this Force is the Divine itself in the body of its power; in the individual it is a Force for illumination, transformation, purification, for all that has to be done in the yoga.
**Force, the Mother's** — the higher Force of the Divine that descends from above to transform the nature; the Divine Force which works to remove the ignorance and change the nature into the divine nature.

**Inconscient (Incinscience), the** — the most involved state of the Superconscience; all powers of the Superconscience progressively evolve and emerge out of the Inconscient, the first emergence being Matter.

**inner being (consciousness)** — the inner being or consciousness means the inner mind, inner vital, inner physical and behind them the psychic which is their inmost being; also called the subliminal (being); sometimes the vital and the mental beings are referred to as inner beings in relation to the physical being.

**inner mind** — that which lies behind the surface mind (our ordinary mentality); this inner or subliminal mind senses directly all the things of the mind-plane, is open to the action of a world of mental forces, and can feel the ideative and other imponderable influences which act upon the material world and the life-plane but which at present we can only infer and cannot directly experience.

**inner physical** — the physical part of the inner being.

**inner vital** — the vital part of the inner being.

**Mantra** — set words or sounds having a spiritual significance or power; sacred syllable, name or mystic formula.

**mental, the** — *see* **mind**

**mental plane** — the world of mental existence above the vital plane or life-world.

**mind (the mental)** — "mind" and "mental" connote specially that part of the nature which has to do with cognition and intelligence, with ideas, with mental or thought perceptions, the reactions of thought to things, with the truly mental movements and formations, mental vision and will, etc. that are part of man's intelligence. The ordinary mind has three main parts: mind proper, vital mind, and physical mind.

The **mind proper** is divided into three parts: the thinking mind or intellect, concerned with ideas and knowledge in their own right; the dynamic mind, concerned with the putting out of mental forces for the realisation of the ideas; and the externalising mind, concerned with the expression of ideas in life.

The **vital mind** or desire mind is a mind of dynamic will, action, desire; it is occupied with force and achievement and satisfaction and possession, with enjoyment and suffering, giving and taking, growth and expansion, etc.

The **physical mind** is that part of the mind which is concerned with physical things only; limited by the physical view and experience of things, it mentalises the experience brought by the contact of outward life and things, but does not go beyond that. The mechanical mind, closely connected with the physical mind, goes on repeating without use whatever has happened.

Overtopping the ordinary mind, hidden in our own superconscient parts, there are higher ranges of Mind, gradations of spiritualised mind leading to the Supermind. In ascending order they are: Higher Mind, Illumined Mind, Intuition and Overmind.

**Nature** — the outer or executive side of the Conscious Force which forms and moves the worlds; Nature is physical, vital, mental.

**plane (of being or consciousness)** — a world or realm of existence.

**physical consciousness** — the physical mind, the physical vital as well as the body consciousness proper.

**physical mind** — *see under* **mind**

**Prakriti** — Nature; mind, life and body constitute the Prakriti of an individual.

**psyche** — the soul; spark of the Divine before it has evolved into an individualised being; the divine essence in the individual. In the course of the evolution, the soul grows and evolves in the form of a soul-personality, the psychic being. *See also* **psychic being** *and* **soul**.

**psychic, the** — psychic being, the term is sometimes used for the psyche or soul. *See also* **psyche** *and* **psychic being**.

**psychic being** — the divine portion in the individual which evolves from life to life, growing by its experiences until it becomes a fully conscious being. The term "soul" is often used as a synonym for "psychic being", but strictly speaking, the soul is the undifferentiated psychic essence, whereas the psychic being is the individualised soul-personality developed by the psychic essence in the course of evolution. *See also* **psychic, the**.

**Sachchidananda (Sat-Chit-Ananda)** — the One Divine Being with a triple aspect of Existence (Sat), Consciousness (Chit) and Delight (Ananda). God is Sachchidananda; He manifests Himself as infinite Existence of which the essentiality is Consciousness, of which again the essentiality is bliss, is self-delight.

**Sadhana** — the practice of yoga.

**Samadhi** (*samādhi*) — yogic trance (in which the mind acquires the capacity of withdrawing from its limited waking activities into freer and higher states of consciousness).

**Subconscient (subconscience, subconscious), the** — the subconscient or subconscious of the individual is that submerged part of his being in which there is no waking conscious and coherent thought, will, feeling or organised reaction, but which yet receives obscurely the impressions of all things and stores them up; from it too all sorts of stimuli, of persistent habitual movements can surge up into dream or into the waking state. In the ordinary man the subconscient includes the larger part of the vital being and the physical mind and the secret body consciousness. It is not to be confused with the subliminal: the subconscient is a *nether* diminished consciousness, the subliminal is an *inner* consciousness larger than our surface existence.

**subconscience, the** — *see* **subconscient, the**.

**subconscious, the** — *see* **subconscient, the**.

**subliminal, the** — the inner being, taken in its entirety of inner mind, inner life, inner physical, with the soul or psychic entity supporting them. The subliminal in man is the largest part of his nature; it is not subconscient, but conscient and greater than the waking consciousness. The subconscient is that which is *below* the ordinary consciousness, the subliminal that which is *behind* and supports it.

**subliminal being** — *see* **inner being**.

**subtle-physical, the** — *see* **inner physical**.

*svapna-samādhi* — dream trance.

**Tamas** — the quality that hides or darkness; the quality of ignorance, inertia and obscurity, of incapacity and inaction; the force of inconscience. Tamas is one of the three Gunas or modes of Nature.

**Upanishads** — a class of Hindu sacred writings, regarded as the source of the Vedanta philosophy.

**vital plane** — the life-world or desire-world which exists above the material universe.

**vital, the** — the life-nature made up of desires, sensations, feelings, passions, energies of action and of all the play of possessive and other related instincts, such as anger, fear, greed, lust, etc. The vital has three main parts:

    **higher vital**: the mental vital and emotional vital taken together. The mental vital gives a mental expression by thought, speech or otherwise to the emotions, desires, passions, sensations or other movements of the vital being; the emotional vital is the seat of various feelings, such as love, joy, sorrow, hatred and the rest.

    **central vital** or **vital proper**: dynamic, sensational and passionate, it is the seat of the stronger vital longings and reactions, such as ambition, pride, fear, love of fame, attractions and repulsions, desires and passions of various kinds and the field of many vital energies.

    **lower vital**: made up of the smaller movements of human life-desire and life-reactions, it is occupied with small desires and feelings, such as food desire, sexual desire, small likings, dislikings, vanity, quarrels, love of praise, anger at blame, little wishes of all kinds, etc.

**Yoga** — the discipline by which one seeks consciously and deliberately to realise union with the Divine or, more generally, to attain a higher consciousness.

# REFERENCES

Passages in this book, serially numbered 1-121, have been extracted from: (1) Volumes of Sri Aurobindo Birth Centenary Library (1970-1973) listed under (a); (2) Volumes of Collected Works of the Mother (1972-1987) listed under (b); (3) *Elements of Yoga* (EoY) by Sri Aurobindo (2nd Edition 2001). All the aforementioned books have been published by Sri Aurobindo Ashram, Pondicherry.

## (a) Sri Aurobindo Birth Centenary Library (SABCL)

| Vol. | Title |
|------|-------|
| 15 | *Social and Political Thought* |
| 19 | *The Life Divine — Book Two Part Two* |
| 20 | *The Synthesis of Yoga — Parts One and Two* |
| 21 | *The Synthesis of Yoga — Parts Three and Four* |
| 22 | *Letters on Yoga — Part One* |
| 23 | *Letters on Yoga — Parts Two and Three* |
| 24 | *Letters on Yoga — Part Four* |

## (b) Collected Works of the Mother (CWM)

| Vol. | Title |
|------|-------|
| 3 | *Questions and Answers* |
| 4 | *Questions and Answers 1950-51* |
| 5 | *Questions and Answers 1953* |
| 6 | *Questions and Answers 1954* |
| 7 | *Questions and Answers 1955* |
| 8 | *Questions and Answers 1956* |
| 9 | *Questions and Answers 1957-58* |
| 10 | *On Thoughts and Aphorisms* |
| 12 | *On Education* |
| 14 | *Words of the Mother* |
| 15 | *Words of the Mother* |
| 16 | *Some Answers from the Mother* |
| 17 | *More Answers from the Mother* |

# REFERENCES

References are given below in an abbreviated form. The initial numeral is the serial number of the passage in this book located at the end of each passage. This is followed by the abbreviated title of the series (SABCL or CWM), followed by the volume number and the page number(s) where the passage occurs. For example:

1. CWM: 7:133 indicates that passage 1 is to be found in Collected Works of the Mother, Volume 7, p. 133.

**Sleep — Doorway to
  Worlds Within**

1. CWM 7:133
2. CWM 16:377
3. SABCL 24:1486
4. SABCL 24:1486
5. SABCL 24:1597
6. SABCL 24:1487
7. CWM 16:385
8. SABCL 24:1491
9. SABCL 23:898-99
10. SABCL 24:1493
11. SABCL 24:1482-83
12. SABCL 24:1483-84
13. EoY, pp. 71-72
14. SABCL 24:1485
15. CWM 3:16
16. CWM 4:107-08
17. SABCL 18:422
18. SABCL 23:1023-24
19. CWM: 3:15
20. SABCL 24:1500
21. CWM 15:140
22. SABCL 24:1499

23. CWM 4:192-93
24. CWM 17:150
25. EoY, p. 70
26. SABCL 24:1492
27. CWM 4:126-28
28. EoY, p.70
29. EoY, p.71
30. SABCL 24:1485
31. CWM 4:62-63
32. CWM 16:376
33. SABCL 18:426
34. SABCL 18:423-25

**Dreams and Dream-
  Experiences**

35. SABCL 24:1487
36. SABCL 24:1500
37. SABCL 9:341
38. SABCL 24:1597
39. SABCL 24:1490-91
40. SABCL 24:1492
41. SABCL 9:447-48
42. SABCL 26:362
43. SABCL 24:1322-23

44. SABCL 24:1490
45. SABCL 24:1498
46. SABCL 24:1487
47. CWM 6:147
48. CWM 16:317
49. SABCL 24:1488-89
50. CWM 15:329-30
51. SABCL 24:1496
52. CWM 15:341-42
53. CWM 16:277
54. CWM 3:47
55. SABCL 24:1500
56. EoY, p. 73
57. CWM 16:408
58. CWM 7:108-09
59. CWM 6:142-43
60. SABCL 24:1492-93
61. SABCL 24:1489-90
62. CWM 10:125-26
63. CWM 7:129
64. CWM 4:149
65. CWM 15:348-49

**Remembering and Under-
standing Dreams**

66. SABCL 24: 1494
67. CWM 5:37-39
68. SABCL 24:1493-94
69. SABCL 24:1494-95
70. SABCL 24:1494
71. CWM 7:67
72. EoY, p. 72
73. CWM 15:143
74. CWM 4:319-21

75. CWM 5:28-29
76. SABCL 24:1493
77. SABCL 24:1503
78. SABCL 24:1503
79. CWM 4:108
80. CWM 7:123-24
81. SABCL 24:1498
82. SABCL 24:1496
83. SABCL 24:1502
84. SABCL 24:1497
85. CWM 4:107
86. CWM 16:261-62
87. EoY, pp. 72-73

**Sleep, Dreams and Sadhana**

88. SABCL 24:1480
89. CWM 15:141
90. SABCL 24:1480
91. EoY, *p. 71*
92. SABCL 24:1487-88
93. SABCL 24:1504
94. CWM 3:14-15
95. CWM 16:228
96. CWM 4:62
97. CWM 4:61-62
98. CWM 14:389
99. SABCL 24:1479
100. SABCL 24: 1485-86
101. SABCL 24:1479-80
102. SABCL 24:1481-82
103. SABCL 24:1658
104. SABCL 24:1481
105. SABCL 24:1481
106. SABCL 23:1017

107. CWM 7:119-22
108. SABCL 24:1478
109. CWM 15:140
110. CWM 15:142-43
111. SABCL 24:1481-82
112. CWM 16:266-67
113. CWM 16:400
114. SABCL 24:1482

115. CWM 7:125
116. CWM 15:351-52
117. CWM 15:399-401
118. CWM 7:65-67
119. CWM 16:357-58
120. CWM 2:35
121. SABCL 24:1481

# INDEX